P9-DBL-964

FamilyFun
Homemade
Holidays

Edited by Deanna F. Cook and the
experts at **FamilyFun** magazine

FamilyFun
Homemade Holidays

FAMILYFUN

EDITORS
Deanna F. Cook
and Alexandra Kennedy

MANAGING EDITOR
Barbara Findlen

ASSISTANT EDITOR
Grace Ganssle

EDITORIAL ASSISTANT
Jean Graham

COPY EDITORS
Julia Lynch and
Paula Noonan

CONTRIBUTING
EDITORS
Dawn Chipman,
Ann Hallock, and
Gregory Lauzon

PICTURE EDITOR
Mark Mantegna

PRODUCTION
Jennifer Mayer and
Dana Stiepock

TECHNOLOGY
COORDINATOR
Tom Lepper

IMPRESS INC.
CREATIVE DIRECTOR
Hans Teensma

DESIGN DIRECTOR
Carolyn Eckert

PROJECTS DIRECTOR
Lisa Newman

DESIGN ASSOCIATE
Pamela Glaven

ART ASSISTANT
Jen Darcy

This book is dedicated to the readers of *FamilyFun* magazine.

All of the ideas in this book first appeared in *FamilyFun* magazine. *FamilyFun* is a division of the Walt Disney Publishing Group. To order a subscription, call 800-289-4849.

The staffs of *FamilyFun* and Impress, Inc. conceived and produced *FamilyFun Homemade Holidays* at 244 Main Street, Northampton, Massachusetts 01060, in collaboration with Disney Editions, 114 Fifth Avenue, New York, New York 10011.

ISBN 0-7868-5360-3

Special thanks to the following *FamilyFun* magazine writers for contributing their homemade holiday ideas: Barbara Albright, Rani Arbo, Beth Barr, Lynn Bertrand, Deb Geigis Berry, Heidi Boyd, Jennifer Bragg, Marie Cecchini, Joan Cirillo, Maryellen Kennedy Duckett, Suzanne Elliot, Ronnie Citron-Fink, Susan Gelotte, Phoebe Graber, Carol Green, Cathryn Harding, Jenifer Harms, Jessica Hastreiter, Ken Haedrich, Danyelle Heafey, Joni Hilton, Nancy Mades, Shoshana Marchand, Charlotte Meryman, Susan Milord, Catherine Newman, Jodi Picoult, Andrea Davis Pinkney, Barbara Prest, Leslie Garisto Pfaff, Constance Ryskamp, Jonathan Sapers, Kathy Schultz, Maryellen Sullivan, Emily Todd, Laura Torres, and Lynn Zimmerman.

We also would like to thank the following stylists: Bonnie Anderson/Team, Grace Arias, Bonnie Aunchman-Goudreau, Heidi Boyd, Catherine Callahan, Jen Darcy, Carel Di Grappa, Bettina Fisher, Sherri Haab, Jessica Hastreiter, Jee Levin, Sara Mills Broffman, Marie Piraino, Karen Quatsoe, Abigail Rieser, Edwina Stevenson, Janet Street, Maryellen Sullivan, Laura Torres, Stacy Webb, and Lynn Zimmerman.

We also extend our gratitude to *FamilyFun*'s many creative readers who shared with us their ideas for celebrating the holidays. Thanks to Lorraine C. Al-Rawi, Lori Bagnoli, Kim & Ric Brown, Dottie Burke, Jami Champagne, Mindy Starns Clark, Barbara Console, Mindy d'Arbeloff, Emily Edgerley, ReGenna Gamblin, Barbara Hampson, Kim Johnson, Rhonda Johnstone, Jacqueline Kremer, Janna Kuklis, Lauri Levenberg, Carol Marion, Maureen Mollette, Nancy Morrison, Lisa J. Nix, Nancy Ojeda, Amy & Toni Persechini, Tammy Pryor, Kimberly Rivera, Connie Singer, Rebecca Skolnick, Connie Stewart, Kelly Vogt, Amy Waltz, Kenneth Waterman, and Julia Wilson.

This book would not have been possible without the talented *FamilyFun* magazine staff, who edited and art-directed the holiday articles for the magazine from 1993 to 2002. We also would like to thank our partners at Disney Editions, especially Wendy Lefkon and Jody Revenson.

About the editors:
Deanna F. Cook is the manager of creative development of *FamilyFun* magazine and the editor of the *FamilyFun* book series from Disney Editions as well as the author of *The Kids' Multicultural Cookbook* from Williamson. She and her husband, Doug, celebrate the holidays in their Northampton, Massachusetts, home with their two girls, Ella and Maisie.

Alexandra Kennedy is the editorial director of *FamilyFun* and *Disney Magazine*. She, her husband, and their two young sons live in Northampton, Massachusetts.

Contents

Present Scents,
page 93

Swirl-a-balls, page 17

Snowmen Sticks,
page 52

Pinecone Trees, page 9

Ringing in the Holidays

AS THE MOTHER of two lively little girls, one of my favorite times of the year is the holidays. Every day in December, I get to relive the magic of my own childhood at Christmastime with Ella, five, and Maisie, two — decorating sugar-cookie Santas with red sprinkles, stringing cranberries and popcorn for the tree, and crafting gifts for grandparents and teachers. Like myself as a child, my kids can't seem to get enough holiday activities.

Fortunately, I have a lot of ideas at my fingertips. At *FamilyFun* magazine, we have collected, developed, and tested hundreds of holiday projects, from homemade ornaments to gifts kids can make. Each of the ideas you'll find here are relatively easy to pull off — and they allow plenty of room for a child's personal touch. Some of the ideas are as simple as making pipe cleaner and bead ornaments for the tree on page 28. Others are more ambitious, such as crafting a reindeer wreath for your front door on page 26. We also feature projects that can be built on year after year, such as the handprint Family Tree Skirt on page 19.

Our collection of great holiday ideas comes from a community of parents just like you — the readers of *FamilyFun* magazine, the mothers and fathers on our staff, and our contributing writers and crafters. When you look through this book, you'll see that many of the projects tell the story of one family's holiday traditions. For instance, the advent calendar on page 20 was a gift from editor Ann Hallock's grandmother that her son Nat will now use to count down the days until Christmas. The Skolnicks, readers of *FamilyFun,* bring their family together every year by making creative Hanukkah decorations and playing the dreidel game on page 61. And writer Emily Todd has baked and decorated Gingerbread Men on page 36 with her sisters every Christmas Eve for the past 25 years.

As all of our contributors can attest, making something with your hands adds richness and importance to the holidays. While our kids craft gifts and cook goodies, we are teaching them the true meaning of the holiday season — and the joy of giving. And with each felt ornament, we create holiday memories that will last for years.

I know it won't be long before my girls are asking me, "What projects are we going to do this year?" Maybe we'll make the Christmas Card Stamps out of their artwork on page 91 or the Gingerbread Family Kit on page 37. But one thing I know for sure, we will make our holidays homemade.

— Deanna F. Cook

Baby Sock Snowman, page 15

CHAPTER ONE

Holiday Crafts & Decorations

FOR MANY FAMILIES, unpacking boxes of holiday decorations is like flipping through the pages of a family scrapbook. When we see the felt photo ornaments, pipe cleaner stars, and faded patchwork angels, we remember the year they were made by our children. In many ways, these simple decorations show us where we've been — and how we've grown.

To add to your family's ranks of homemade decorations, we present 30 pages of our favorite ideas. Each one of our crafts is fun to make and requires only basic materials and an afternoon of free time. That means that even in this hectic season, you and your children have a good shot at making, and actually finishing, a few holiday projects together. And when you do, you may discover — as so many readers of *FamilyFun* magazine have — that something put together in minutes can last for years.

When you're ready to make decorations this year, review the following tips first.

Make a list and check it twice. At the beginning of the holiday season, take a moment to peruse this chapter with your children and pick out a few crafts that you like best (and that are age-appropriate). Then use our materials lists to jot down the items you'll need to make

them. Many of the materials can be found around the house — and the rest can be picked up at your local art supply store. Once you have all the supplies on hand, you'll be prepared for an impromptu crafting session.

Encourage creativity. When making any of our holiday crafts with your children, steer toward a finished product, but emphasize the process. The end result, after all, is no more important than the steps that lead up to it. Encourage your kids to customize our crafts — they might decorate the Paper Gingerbread Village on page 9 so it resembles the houses in your neighborhood or craft the Beaded Beauties on page 28 with their favorite shapes and colors.

Start a holiday crafting tradition. Find a holiday craft you and your kids would like to do year after year, such as making ornaments or creating gifts. Over the years, this activity will become a ritual — something you and your kids will look forward to as much as opening the presents under the tree.

Save your holiday crafts. Many of the crafts in this chapter will weather several years in a box. If you plan to keep your child's decorations, be sure to label them with his or her name and the date. Take photographs of the crafts that won't last — or are too large to keep.

Tiny Tree, page 25

Cardboard Gingerbread Cookies

Squirtable tubes of puffy fabric paint and a blow-dryer are the star attractions of this quick and easy craft. We used the paint like icing to decorate our cardboard cookies, and we found that the containers kept the process surprisingly mess-free, even in the hands of a four- or five-year-old. The kids thought it was especially neat to use a hair dryer to make the paint puff up after it was dry.

MATERIALS

    Corrugated cardboard
    Cookie cutters
    Craft knife
    Puffy fabric paint
    Blow-dryer
    Ribbon

Trace around cookie cutters on cardboard and cut out the "cookies" with a craft knife (a parent's job). Then, decorate with puffy fabric paint. Let the paint dry a few hours, if possible, then blow-dry and watch it puff! (If you are doing this craft with guests, have them paint at the start of the activity so they can blow-dry before they leave.) Punch a hole in the top and thread with a ribbon for hanging.

Tip: When you cut out the "cookie," you don't have to cut all the way through the cardboard at once — go over the cutting line a couple of times.

Holiday Hustle

"On the Sunday after Thanksgiving, my husband, our two children, and I kicked off the Christmas season with a special family party. We had a picnic in front of the fireplace, played Christmas carols, and talked about past holidays. I gave Drew, nine, and Emily, seven, each a December calendar with crayons and stickers, while I brought the family calendar and a stack of invitations and announcements for the coming month. We took turns saying which activities we most wanted to do, wrote them down, and decorated the dates. Together, we picked days to put up our tree, make gingerbread houses, and go caroling. As the month got more hectic, the kids could glance at their calendars to see when their activities would take place. Helping with the plans made all of us feel like we had more control over the busy holiday schedule."

— Julia Wilson
Omaha, Nebraska

Paper Gingerbread Village

Made from brown paper bags and puffy paint, this gingerbread town is a breeze to construct, and it has a much longer shelf life than the edible cookie version.

MATERIALS

- Brown paper lunch bags
- Newspaper
- Colored paper
- Craft scissors or pinking shears (optional)
- White puffy paint and blow dryer
- Glue stick and tape
- Colored markers

Have your child stuff each bag about half full with newspaper, then fold down the top so that it resembles a pitched roof. If you prefer a colored-paper roof, cut out a rectangle that's at least double the size of the folded top. Fold the rectangle in half, as shown below. For a decorative touch, trim the lower edges of the roof with craft scissors or pinking shears. Use puffy paint to create shingle lines, then blow-dry.

Next, cut windows and doors from colored paper and glue them onto the houses. Use the puffy paint or colored markers to add trim and other decorative details.

For a chimney, fold a 1½- by 5½-inch strip of colored paper into a rectangle and tape the ends together. Snip small triangles from the bottoms of two opposite sides. Then paint on brick lines and set the chimney atop the roof peak.

Christmas Choir

Arranged on a windowsill or mantel, this caroling trio is just the prop to spread holiday cheer. These songsters also make a fun addition to the Paper Gingerbread Village.

MATERIALS

- Tempera paint and paintbrushes
- 1 toilet paper tube
- 1 paper towel tube, cut into 2 different lengths
- Colored paper (for faces and mittens)
- Black marker and pink pencil
- Sheet music (from a songbook or gift wrap)
- Glue
- 3 child's socks
- String or raffia

Paint the tubes and set them aside to dry. From the colored paper, cut out oval face shapes and draw on eyes and mouths with the marker. Use the pink pencil to color rosy cheeks. Cut out paper mittens for each caroler too.

From the sheet music, trim three small rectangles and fold each in half to resemble a mini songbook. Glue the faces onto the tubes. Then glue a songbook between each pair of mittens and glue the mittens to the tubes.

For hats, trim the feet off the socks and discard them. Fold an end of each sock tube into a cuff and stretch it onto a caroler's head. Tie the hat closed with string or raffia.

PINECONE TREES

Looking for a quick holiday craft project to bring into your child's school? Try these pinecone Christmas trees, inspired by *FamilyFun* editor Deanna Cook. Deanna and her 5-year-old daughter Ella collected several pinecones from a local nature trail. They brought them into Ella's school classroom along with paint and mini terracotta pots. The kids painted the pinecones green and white and the mini pots their favorite colors. Once the cones were dried, the kids decorated their Christmas trees with glitter glue, mini pom-pom ornaments, and glitter "snow."

Yarn Candy Canes

A neat twist on a classic, these canes are fun to assemble (and they make excellent gifts).

MATERIALS

    2 skeins of DMC Pearl Cotton, one red and one white

    Red pipe cleaners

    8 inches of ½-inch to ⅝-inch ribbon

Open a skein of cotton and snip the loop at each end so you have two bunches; repeat with the other skein. Then take one red bunch and one white bunch and tie them together into a single knot around the end of a pipe cleaner. To make the stripes, twist the two colors around the pipe cleaner and knot the ends together around the other end. Trim the cotton at both ends and trim the pipe cleaner if need be. Bend into a candy cane shape and adorn with a ribbon bow.

Tip: These candy canes were created with fine DMC Pearl Cotton, but younger kids may have an easier time with chenille yarn or cord.

Hanukkah Paper Cones

Imagine seeing these cones on your doorknob or bedpost, brimming with Hanukkah gelt or small gifts. These directions make three.

MATERIALS

    1 piece of heavy paper for inner layer, 14 inches square (try a grocery bag or drawing paper)

    3 pieces of decorative paper for outer layer, 8½ by 11 inches (try rice paper or gift wrap)

    Glue and stapler

    Ribbons and trim

On the heavy paper, use a pencil to draw a circle 14 inches in diameter. Make a mark at the top of the circle.

Next, use a ruler to measure a 12-inch line from that mark to the edge of the circle; make a second mark there. Do the same on the other side of the circle so you have three marks, spaced equally around the circle's circumference (see A). Next, draw straight lines from all three marks into the center and cut along those lines to create three pie slices. Take one slice and trace it onto the wrong side of a piece of the decorative outer paper, adding a half inch extra on all sides (see B). Cut out the decorative paper shape. Glue the heavy inner paper shape onto the wrong side of the decorative paper. Along the rounded edge, snip the decorative paper border every half inch. Fold these flaps onto the inner paper and glue. Then fold the straight sides onto the inner paper and glue.

Now roll the paper into a cone, overlapping the edges 1½ inches at the top, and glue. Add trim at the top and staple ribbon handles to the cone. Fill with treats.

LEND-A-HAND WREATH

Celebrate the gift of giving with this wreath of helping hands. To make the base of the wreath, cut out the middle of a paper plate. Color the remaining circle green with markers or paint. Trace your child's hand on card stock to create a pattern. Using the pattern, cut out hands from green construction paper (make enough hands to equal the number of countdown days). Write one good deed or simple service project on the back of each and set them aside in a basket. Each day, pick a hand from the basket, perform the deed or service, and add it to the wreath (we attached each hand with adhesive Fun-Tak to give the wreath more texture).

Snow Angel

Dressed in a soft, snow-white robe, this angel will look heavenly set on a table or perched atop your Christmas tree.

MATERIALS

- Thin wooden kitchen skewer
- Smooth foam ball (4 inches in diameter)
- Acrylic paint (for face) and paintbrush
- Double-sided foam tape
- Googly eyes
- Red construction paper
- 32-ounce plastic container (yogurt container or soda cup)
- Pushpin
- Polyester quilt batting
- Several gold and silver pipe cleaners
- Small sewing pins
- Gold tinsel or tinsel ribbon (sold on the spool)
- White and pink craft foam
- Gold glitter glue (or gold puffy paint)

Angel face: Push the pointed end of the wooden skewer 2 to 3 inches into the foam ball. Holding the ball by the skewer, paint it so that it is well coated, then prop the skewer in a glass and allow the paint to dry completely. Use double-sided foam tape to attach the googly eyes and a red paper mouth.

Snow-white robe: Turn the plastic container upside down and use the pushpin to make a hole through the center of the bottom (where the skewer will be inserted later). Apply four equally spaced strips of the double-sided tape to the sides of the container (see A). Next, cut long 6-inch-wide strips from the quilt batting. Twist the end of one strip and stick it against the tape near the bottom of the container and begin winding the strip around the container in rows, twisting the batting into a loose roll as you go. When you get to the end of the strip, continue with more strips of batting until the container is completely covered. For trim, wrap gold pipe cleaners around the robe.

Golden curls: Attach the foam head to the body by inserting the blunt end of the skewer through the hole in the container. Then cover the head with curls by pinning strands of tinsel to the foam ball in a zigzag fashion. For a halo, shape a silver pipe cleaner into a circle and twist the ends together. Attach a second pipe cleaner for the halo stem and wrap the lower end around the skewer.

Wings and things: From the white craft foam, cut out a pair of butterfly-like wings and two 8½-inch-long arms. Tape the arms together to form one piece that wraps three quarters of the way around the angel (see B). Use glitter glue to trim the wings and sleeves. Once the glue is dry, use the double-sided tape to attach the arms to the batting and then the wings to the back

of the arms. Cut out pink foam mitten-shaped hands and tape them to the inside ends of the sleeves. For the finishing touch, cut out a small song-book from the red construction paper and adorn it with glitter glue. Use more double-sided tape to attach the book to the angel's hands.

Family Photo Ornament

For most families, ornaments are more than decorations; they're memories in miniature, especially the homemade creations, whose cockeyed charm so perfectly captures the creativity of your child at a particular moment in time.

This year, why not take the idea a step further and let your kids put a little bit of themselves into the decorations — literally. Each child gets to choose a photo of himself or herself to incorporate in an ornament, which can be as simple as a Popsicle-stick frame or as sophisticated as a decoupaged Styrofoam ball. The only requirement is that the finished product reflect the personality of its maker (and include the year in which it was made). Your kids will have fun comparing their faces over the years, and you'll love seeing your tree transformed into a virtual family album.

Faux Fireplace

For those whose Christmas holiday lacks a hearth by which to hang stockings with care, this cardboard fireplace makes a great stand-in.

MATERIALS

Four 18-inch square boxes and two
    28- by 20- by 5-inch rectangular
    boxes (generally sold at mailing
    service and supply stores)
Brown paper packing tape
Newspaper
Acrylic paint (red, brown, cream,
    black, and white)
Paper plates
Large rectangular sponge

The Story of the Stocking

According to one legend, the practice of hanging up Christmas stockings started when Saint Nicholas tried to help out a man who needed a wedding dowry for his daughter. While the family slept, he tossed a bag of gold through the window, and it landed in one of the girls' stockings, which had been hung up to dry. For fun, your kids can reenact the legend. Stuff an empty juice can into the top of a woolen sock and hang it from a doorknob. Then, all the family members can take turns trying their luck at tossing pennies into the can from a few feet away.

Small rag
Sheet of gray paper (at least
    20 inches square)

Build the hearth: Assemble the four square boxes. Leaving one top flap open on each box, seal the other flap edges with packing tape. Then stack two boxes on end with the free flaps on the same side and tape the flaps together. Next, tape all the seams and edges to create a smooth surface for painting. Do the same with the other two boxes. Now set the two stacks side by side so that the open flaps meet in the middle. Tape the flaps together to form the hearth's back wall.

Paint the bricks: Cover your work area with newspaper. Squeeze some red, brown, and cream acrylic paint onto a paper plate. Dampen the sponge and then coat its surface with paint by blotting the different colors to achieve a mottled effect. Use it to print rows of bricks on the hearth, recoating it with paint as needed.

Make the mantel: Assemble the two rectangular boxes and tape them together end to end. Squeeze black and white paint onto a second paper plate. Dampen the rag, dip it in both shades of paint, and apply the paint to the mantel in swirls to create a marbled gray surface. Once dry, set the mantel on the hearth and slip the gray paper in place for the fireplace floor.

◆ FAMILYFUN READER TRADITION

Yule Logs

"It always seems sad to take down our Christmas tree, but my family found a way to save a keepsake of each one. I saw off a 1/2-inch slice of the trunk, and we all take part in decorating it. Billy, twelve, and Sean, nine, paint on the date and add a memento of the year. We drill a hole in the top and string through a piece of yarn to make it an ornament for next year's tree."

— Dottie Burke
New Orleans, Louisiana

Paper Cup Menorah

This simple, faux menorah makes it a cinch for little ones, or *bubbelahs* as they say in Yiddish, to light their own candles during the Hanukkah holiday.

MATERIALS

Yellow and orange tempera paint
Paintbrush
9 flat wooden craft spoons
Craft knife
Twelve 9-ounce paper cups

Have your child paint the wider ends of the wooden craft spoons (fronts and backs) to resemble yellow-orange flames. Meanwhile, use the craft knife to cut a ¾-inch slit in the bottoms of nine of the paper cups (a parent's job). Cut the bottoms out of the remaining three cups and stack them rims down. Line up the nine cups in a horizontal row, as shown below, placing the middle one atop the stack of three. When it's time, your child can light the menorah by inserting the bottoms of the wooden flames in the holes in the candles.

Snowman Garland

Whether you live in a cold or warm climate, your kids can have fun rounding up these decorative snowmen. String them together, and they look great as a doorway or banister adornment. Or, you can hang them singly as tree ornaments.

MATERIALS

2 different-size jar lids (we used one with a 2-inch diameter and another with a 3-inch diameter)
Cardboard
4 or more 9- by 12-inch sheets of white craft foam
Puffy paint
Ribbon, fleece, and felt
Small pom-poms
Tacky glue
3 yards or more of thin ribbon

Create a template by tracing the jar lids (the smaller one above the larger one, their rims touching) onto the cardboard and cutting out the snowman shape. Use the template to draw snowmen on the craft foam (we fit six per sheet) and cut them out.

Now your child can use puffy paint to add facial features and buttons. While the paint dries, she can cut out ribbon or fleece scarves (about 12 inches long) to tie around the snowmen's necks, as well as brimmed felt hats or stocking caps — complete with a small pom-pom glued to the end — to glue on their heads.

To string the snowmen into a garland, loop the ribbon once around the back of each of their scarves. Keep the loops loose enough that you can slide the snowmen into place along the strand.

Baby Sock Snowman

This is a terrific recycled ornament. Each snowman is made from those baby socks that never really get dirty or wear out. A kindergartner can do this with help, but in a group, this craft is better for older kids.

MATERIALS
1 white and 1 colored baby sock
Batting
String
Fabric or ribbon
Glue or sewing needle and thread
Buttons
Markers
Pipe cleaners
Pom-poms

Fill the foot of a white baby sock with batting. Tie shut just above the ankle with string. Trim off the cuff. Divide the sock ball into the body and head by tying a strip of fabric or ribbon (the scarf) around the sock. To make the hat, gather the colored sock together at the ankle and tie with string. Leave enough string for a hanging loop.

Cut off the foot. Roll up the edge of the sock like a stocking. Glue or sew on the hat. Next, glue or sew on buttons. Draw on the eyes and mouth with markers. Cut a 1-inch piece of pipe cleaner and poke it in for the nose. For earmuffs, wrap a piece of pipe cleaner around the head and tuck the ends under the hat rim. Glue on pom-poms.

Tip: Don't have batting? Use old nylon stockings or cotton balls.

Ornaments Through the Years

"We have a Christmas tradition that makes trimming and untrimming our tree lots of fun. My parents started it when I was young, and my husband and I have continued it with our children, Sarah and Benjamin. We store each ornament in a plastic sandwich bag along with a slip of paper identifying its history: for example, "Pinecone Santa made by Jacqueline in 6th grade" or "Red and green felt tree given to Sarah by Aunt Jean — 1994." The notes help us recall the details that make each ornament special.

After Christmas, we reverse the process. Each person picks an empty bag, reads the tag, then searches the tree to find that ornament. Each year our collection of ornaments and memories grows."

— Jacqueline Kremer
Bozrah, Connecticut

Popsicle-stick Snowflakes

If you're dreaming of a white Christmas, decorate your tree with these easy snowy ornaments. We made the flakes with white buttons, but you can use a variety of decorations (glitter, paint, cotton balls, or whatever supplies you have on hand) to make your flurries.

MATERIALS
White glue
3 Popsicle sticks
White buttons
Fishing line (for hanging)

Place a spot of glue in the center of a Popsicle stick. Place the second stick on top of the first. Then glue on the third stick. The sticks should be stacked in a evenly fanned pattern and resemble a snowflake, as shown.

Set the ornament aside to dry.

Next, glue the white buttons along both sides of the sticks. For a variety of snowflake designs, glue on cotton balls, gems, or silver glitter. Or, simply paint the sticks white. Hang the ornaments with fishing line.

Spool List

Forget about postage to the North Pole. When kids roll their wish lists onto these cute-as-a-button spools, Santa will snap to attention. Be sure to hang them where they'll catch his winking eye — the Christmas tree or the mantel are good bets.

MATERIALS

- Red or green acrylic paint
- Small paintbrush
- Wooden thread spool
- Marker
- Paper strip, cut to fit the width of the spool
- Double-sided tape
- Ribbon (for hanging)
- Self-sticking label

Paint the spool and let it dry. Have your child write her Christmas list on the strip of paper. Roll the paper around the empty spool, using double-sided tape to fasten it, and leave some of the list hanging down (so Santa notices). Thread the ribbon through the spool's center and tie a knot at the top for hanging. Write your child's name on the self-sticking label. Affix it to the ribbon.

Beaded Candles

These beaded "candles" are a creative way to introduce the seven principles of Kwanzaa. Each principle corresponds to a color and has a Swahili name: unity (*umoja*: black), self-determination (*kujichagulia*: red), collective work and responsibility (*ujima*: green), cooperative economics (*ujamaa*: red), purpose (*nia*: green), creativity (*kuumba*: red), and faith (*imani*: green).

MATERIALS

- ¹⁄₂-inch wooden craft cubes
- Red, green, and black acrylic paint
- Small paintbrush
- Glue
- Letter beads
- Yellow oval-shaped beads
- Ribbon

Count out the number of cubes you need for each candle (five for *imani*, for example). Paint the wooden cubes in the appropriate colors and let them dry. Glue the cubes together, remembering to glue the top cube so that the hole faces out for threading the ribbon (if the cubes don't have holes, you can glue the ribbon between the top two cubes). Use the letter beads to glue the name of the principle to the stack of cubes. Glue a yellow bead on top for a flame, thread with the ribbon, and hang.

Wired Star

Although cookie cutters are best known for their work in the kitchen, they can also play a role in decorating your family's Christmas tree. Here's how you and your kids can whip up a batch of shiny holiday ornaments with the old kitchen helper.

MATERIALS

- 18-gauge gold-colored wire
- Wire cutters
- Star cookie cutter
- 20- to 24-gauge colored wire
- Ribbon (for hanging)

To make an ornament, wrap one end of a 3-foot length of the 18-gauge wire around the pencil to form a hanging loop. With the loop at the top of a star cookie cutter, press the wire twice around the perimeter of the cookie cutter to form a star shape, twisting it around the hanging loop and using wire cutters (a parent's job) to snip off any excess. Remove the cookie cutter.

Now your child can complete the ornament by wrapping the wire outline with lengths of the 20- to 24-gauge wire, as shown, securing the ends in place by wrapping them around the cookie cutter outline. Finally, tie a hanging ribbon to the loop, and your ornament is ready for display.

Swirl-a-balls

These ornaments are so much more than the sum of their parts: a flash of holiday alchemy transforms inexpensive glass globes and a few dropperfuls of paint into marbled masterpieces.

MATERIALS

- Clear glass ball ornaments (available at craft stores)
- Acrylic or tempera paint
- Paper cups
- Plastic eyedroppers
- Ornament hooks

Remove the tops from the ornaments (a parent's job). You may want to inspect the top of the ornament for stray glass threads and smooth them with the side of a toothpick.

Pour the paint into the cups, one color per cup, and stir a little water into each until it reaches the consistency of heavy cream. Put an eyedropper in each cup.

To decorate a ball, have your child squirt a few drops of paint into it and swirl before adding another color. Experiment with dribbling paint down the sides or squirting it right into the bottom and tipping the ball upside down over a cup. (Most designs look great, but if a child is really unhappy with his or her ball, you can swirl the inside of the ornament with hot water and start over.)

Dry the balls upside down, perched on paper cups. Replace the tops when the ornaments are dry. Hang on the tree.

Clay Crèche

Using clay and twigs, you and your children can recreate the humble Nativity scene. Before starting, knead the clay to soften it and rid it of air bubbles.

MATERIALS

Polymer clay (we recommend Sculpey III)
Markers
Cardboard
Glue
Twigs and Spanish moss
Popsicle sticks
White paint and paintbrush

Help your child sculpt Mary, Joseph, Jesus, a sheep, donkey, angel, shepherd, and Magi out of the clay, as shown. Roll log shapes for their bodies and round shapes for their heads and hands. For veils, beards, and crowns, roll out thin sheets of clay on waxed paper. Cut out the shape with a knife (parents only), peel it off the paper, and attach to the bodies (use a toothpick if necessary). Bake the figures according to package directions. Once cool, draw on faces with markers.

Construct a stable out of cardboard. Glue twigs and Spanish moss on the roof and Popsicle sticks on the floor. Paint the crèche white. Add a clay star.

Stamped Dough Medallions

Can your angels ever make too many ornaments for your tree? We thought not, so we came up with this craft that can yield as many varieties as you have cookie stamps. We suggest breaking the project into two: make and bake the dough on one day, then paint the ornaments on another day.

MATERIALS

4 cups of all-purpose flour
1 cup of salt
1 1/2 cups of water
Cookie stamps (available at craft and party stores)
Straw
Acrylic paint
Ribbon (for hanging)

To make the dough, mix the flour, salt, and water in a large bowl. Knead well and add more water or flour until you can form into a ball. (Makes enough for 25 ornaments.)

Make a 1-inch ball of dough and smash it with a cookie stamp. Use a straw to poke a hole for hanging. (Poke holes in the tops and bottoms of the disks if you want to attach them to each other.) Heat the oven to 300° and bake for 1 to 1½ hours. Let the ornaments dry for a few days, then paint.

Tip: To make them last, seal the ornaments with a shiny coat of polyurethane spray (adults) or Mod Podge (kids).

pieces together.
(For a moon, use notched circles.)
Thread fishing line through the tops and hang them above the scene.

Plant trees: It wouldn't be a forest without pines. Again, start with like shapes. Notch one from the top to the center and the other from the bottom to the center. Then fit the two together.

Let it snow: Now your child can set up his forest on a sheet of cardboard covered with drifts of faux snow.

✻ TABLETOP DECORATION

Frosty and Friends

No matter how low the mercury falls, it never gets too cold to play in this snowy enchanted forest. Made from thin sheets of craft foam (ask for Foamies at your local craft or art supply store) or poster board, the pieces are a cinch to assemble and virtually unbreakable, unlike many tabletop figurines.

MATERIALS
Craft foam or poster board (a variety of colors)
Colored markers or paints
Fishing line
Faux snow

Round up some animals: Once your child has decided which creatures he'd like to populate his forest, help him sketch the parts of each figure on the foam or poster board. Begin by outlining the animal's torso with only its head and tail attached. Next, draw two pairs of legs (and a set of antlers, if appropriate) separate from the rest of the body.

Cut out the individual pieces with scissors and then snip narrow notches in the top of each set of legs and the bottom of the torso, as shown. Fit the pieces together so the animal will stand on its own. Use the same method to attach the antlers. Add eyes (or stripes on a raccoon's or skunk's tail) with colored markers or paints.

Build a snowman: Cut out two matching foam snowmen. Notch one cutout from the head to the middle of its belly and the other from the bottom to the middle of its belly, as shown. Fit both pieces together. Now cut out a notched top hat and carrot nose and attach them to the snowman. For a scarf, cut out a wavy ribbon shape with one curved end. Cut off the curved end about 1 inch from the edge, then notch the cut edge on both pieces of the scarf and fit them onto the snowman's neck. Draw on coal eyes and a mouth.

Find a constellation: To make stars and a moon, start with pairs of matching shapes. Notch one cutout from the center of a point and the matching star from between two points. Then fit the

Advent Calendar

When she was a girl, *FamilyFun* editor Ann Hallock received an Advent calendar from her grandmother that inspired the one pictured here. The ornaments, made from buttons, beads, and figurines, came with instructions: "Put an ornament in each of the calendar's pockets and hang one every day until Christmas."

MATERIALS

- 24-by 36-inch piece of white fleece
- Red, white, and green thread
- Pins and sewing needle
- Drawing paper and pencil
- 15- by 18-inch piece of green fleece
- 6 red pipe cleaners
- 24 faux pearl buttons
- 1 star-shaped button
- 2 17-inch dowels, 1¼-inch diameter
- 1 20-inch red cord
- 4 wooden beads with ¼-inch hole
- Trinkets, such as beads or plastic figurines
- Gold cord for hanging

Background: Cut an 18- by 36-inch rectangle out of the white fleece. Hem the long sides ½ inch. To make dowel sleeves, turn the top and bottom edges under 1 inch and stitch.

Tree: On paper, sketch a Christmas tree within a 15- by 18-inch rectangle, and cut it out. Pin the tree pattern to the green fleece and cut it out. Pin the treetop to the white fleece about 2½ inches from the top of the background. Center the tree, pin in place, and sew.

Pockets: Cut four 2- by 13½-inch rectangles from the white fleece. Pin the bottom pocket 2 inches from the bottom edge and 2¼ inches from each side. Sew along the pocket's bottom edge, then its sides, leaving the top of the pocket open. Mark off five 2¼-inch intervals on the pocket with pins. Sew five vertical lines dividing the long pocket into six 2¼-inch-wide pockets. Repeat for the three other long pockets,

leaving ½-inch space between each row.

Numbers: Cut the pipe cleaners into sections, making sixteen 1-inch sections for the ones and fours, and twenty-five 2-inch sections for the other numbers. Bend into numbers, then sew them in place.

Finishing touches: Sew the pearl buttons on the tree and the star on the treetop. Insert the dowels into the

sleeves at top and bottom. Stitch a loop at each end of the red cord and slip it over the top dowel ends. Glue the four wooden beads onto the dowel ends.

Ornaments: Find 24 plastic figures, beads, or mini decorations around your house, or at craft or toy stores. Or, make them out of magazine scraps, felt, and buttons. Tie a loop of cord around each trinket so it will hang on the calendar.

Countdown to Christmas

One way to shorten the wait for the holidays is with a homemade Advent calendar like this one. Starting with the first day of December, your child gets to snip off a number a day and uncover the treat hidden inside.

MATERIALS

- 25 small treats
- Roll of 2-inch-wide colored tape
- Construction paper or paper grocery bags
- Puffy paint
- Tape or glue
- Rickrack
- Colored yarn

Gather 25 small treats, such as gumball machine prizes, wrapped candy, and trinkets. Cut a 4½-foot length of 2-inch-wide colored tape. Lay the tape sticky side up and place the treats along the length of it, approximately 1 inch apart.

Next, tape together several pieces of construction paper or sections of a paper grocery bag to create a 6-foot-long, 3-inch-wide strip. Place it atop the treat-covered tape and press together the paper and tape around each treat. Trim off any excess paper.

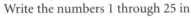

Write the numbers 1 through 25 in

puffy paint on pieces of colored construction paper and cut them out. (We shaped our pieces into green trees, red Christmas balls, and a yellow star.) Starting at the bottom, tape or glue the numbers to the paper strip, one over each treat.

Finally, glue rickrack along the edges of the paper and tape the top of the calendar to a pencil. Tie a length of colored yarn to the ends of the pencil, and your Advent calendar is ready to hang.

PUT ON A BOW TIE

Want to get your child involved with decorating? Ask him to dress up his favorite stuffed animals by tying colorful ribbon around their necks or topping them with Santa hats or red knit caps. Then he can prop them on a sofa or guest bed.

Merry Mice

Whether used as gift tags, hung on the tree, or given as sweet presents all by themselves, these candy mice are sure to cause a stir. Assembly is quick and easy, making them the perfect craft for the hectic holidays.

MATERIALS

- Red felt
- Green felt
- Googly eyes
- Green pom-pom
- 1 candy cane

To make each mouse, cut a 6-inch-long teardrop-shaped body from red felt. Near the center, cut two parallel slits that are 1 inch long and ½ inch apart, as shown. For a pair of ears, cut a 5-inch-long rounded bow-tie shape from green felt.

Now put the mouse together by fitting the ears through the slits in the body. Glue on googly eyes and a pom-pom nose. Finally, add a curly tail by slipping a candy cane beneath the mouse and tucking the straight end between the body and the ears to hold it in place.

Lantern Village

Candlelight shines through the windows of these houses, which are an inexpensive alternative to store-bought villages. Your kids can customize the houses to look like your neighborhood, then arrange them on a mantel.

MATERIALS

- Votive candle and candleholder
- Poster board
- Craft knife
- Construction paper
- Acrylic or puffy paint and paintbrushes
- Glue

 Measure the bottom and one side of your candleholder. On a piece of poster board, sketch a house that is at least 1 inch wider than the holder and 1 inch taller than its base and side combined. Using a craft knife (parents only), cut out the house and a few windows. Your child can decorate it with construction paper and acrylic or puffy paint. When the house is dry, flip it over and set the holder on the house base. Score the line between the house and the base. Fold up the house and attach it to the holder with a dab of glue.

Cardboard Candles

As pretty as they can be, real holiday candles aren't always practical to burn when you have children in the house. For a safe and surprisingly striking alternative, you and your kids can turn paper towel and tissue tubes into an array of candlesticks complete with drips and shimmery flames.

MATERIALS

- Cardboard tubes
- White glue
- Acrylic paint and paintbrush
- Gold foil wrapping paper
- Tape

First, set the cardboard tubes on end, then (here's the fun part) squirt blobs of white glue right from the bottle around the top of each one. Allow the glue to run down the sides to create a dripped-wax effect. Let the glue dry thoroughly (it should look clear when it has). Now brush on a coat or two of acrylic paint over the dried glue and again let the candlesticks dry completely.

Finally, cut a flame shape for each candle from a sheet of gold foil wrapping paper. Attach each flame to its candlestick by taping the lower edge to the inside of the painted tube.

✳ **EASY CRAFT**

ORANGE GLOW

Brighten your dinner table with a fragrant citrus votive candle. On the top of an orange, trace around a tea light candle. Use a knife (parents only) to cut along the line and form a ³/₄-inch-deep hole for the light. Then arrange it on a plate of pine, fir, or holly, where it will last a couple of days.

✳ **TABLETOP DECORATION**

Angel Votive

This shimmery angel is designed to sit on a tabletop. Its wings and skirt cast a warm and flickering glow from a candle.

MATERIALS

Disposable aluminum roasting pan
Hole punch
Votive and candleholder

First, cut out a paper angel to use as a pattern. It's easy if you draw a rectangular base, a triangular skirt, heart-shaped wings, and a round head topped with a narrow strip for a halo. Fold the pattern in half.

Next, cut out the bottom from a disposable aluminum roasting pan, fold it lengthwise, and sandwich it between the folded paper. Trace around the pattern and then cut along the lines.

Punch holes in the aluminum cutout along the fold and the wings. Use a pencil to etch lines in the skirt. Spread open the aluminum angel. Then fold the base to fit under a glass candleholder and fashion the strip above the angel's head into a halo.

✶ EASY ORNAMENT
Golden Girl

Top your tree with this glittery angel, made with glue, string, and gold glitter.

MATERIALS

- 1-liter plastic soda bottle
- String
- White-glue-and-water solution
- Waxed paper
- Cookie sheet
- Gold glitter, round ornament, and tinsel

Cut the bottom off the soda bottle. Dip pieces of string into a white-glue-and-water solution (it should be the consistency of thick cream) and coil them around the entire bottle, starting at the bottom.

On a waxed-paper–lined cookie sheet, shape a long piece of glue-soaked string into an outline of angel wings. Fill in the wings with dipped string coiled into lacy patterns. Before the glue dries, liberally sprinkle glitter on the body and wings. Once they're dry, glue the wings to the body. For the head, glue the ornament, hook down, on top of the bottle. Crown the angel with a gold tinsel halo.

✶ HOME DECORATION
Candy Cane Display

Mounted in a doorway, this oversize display has room for dozens of cards. As if that weren't sweet enough, it's studded with real candy to help your kids appreciate each tiding of joy: when a new card goes up, a candy comes down.

MATERIALS

- 2 pieces of foam core (we used 20- by 30-inch sheets)
- Craft knife
- Duct tape
- 6 yards of 3-inch-wide red satin ribbon
- Thumbtacks or finishing nails
- Oversize red paper clips
- Small wrapped candies

Using a craft knife (parents only), cut the foam core into two 9-inch-wide strips and one candy cane hook, then assemble the sections with duct tape (trim the completed cane to fit in your door frame).

Cut the ribbon stripes so that an inch or so overlaps to the back of the foam candy cane, and tape them in place. Mount the candy cane on the door trim with thumbtacks or finishing nails. Insert paper clips through the wrappers of holiday candies, then clip the candies to the ribbon (you might keep a box of clips handy in case the mail carrier is especially generous).

Elegant Paper Drops

Gorgeous proof of elegance in simplicity, these graceful paper shapes come together with two snaps of a stapler (a perfect job for a kid). They can dress up a window, hang on a tree, or spin in midair from a light fixture or a ribbon.

MATERIALS

- Colorful heavy construction paper 1½ inches wide and at least 12 inches long
- Ruler
- Stapler
- Thin gold cord

Paper drop: Cut two 12-inch strips, two 10-inch strips, and one 8¾-inch strip of paper. Stack them up in this order: 12, 10, 8¾, 10, 12, with one set of ends even. Staple this end. Stack up the other ends evenly (bending the outer strips as needed) and staple.

Heart: Cut two 12-inch strips and two 9½-inch strips. Line them up in this order: 9½, 12, 12, 9½, with one set of ends even. Staple this end. Now bend the unstapled ends into a heart shape, so a small heart lies inside a larger heart (as shown, left). Align the ends and staple together.

Teardrop: Cut two 12-inch strips, two 10½-inch strips, and one 9-inch strip. Line them up in this order: 12, 10½, 9, 10½, 12, with one set of ends even. Staple this end. Next, make a crease ¾ inch from the unstapled ends of the 12- and 10½-inch strips. Finally, align the ends of all the strips and staple them together.

Ornament: To hang each design, knot the end of the gold cord and place it between the loose strips of paper at the top. Staple it all together.

Deck the Doorways

"After moving into a smaller house, my family could no longer put up as large a Christmas tree as we'd always had. To our disappointment, there just wasn't space for all our treasured ornaments. We decided to hang a pine garland over each bedroom door and let each family member choose favorite ornaments to display. My children, Heather, age twelve, and Caleb, age eight, proudly showed them to visiting family and friends — and the garlands gave our whole house a merry look."

— ReGenna Gamblin
Bangs, Texas

★ TABLETOP DECORATION

TINY TREE

Planted in a drift of "snow," this miniature Christmas tree is just right for decorating a child's dresser or nightstand. To set one up, first trim and shape an evergreen clipping so that it resembles a conical tree with a trunk. Fill a glass jar or cup with salt and push the bottom of the tree deep enough into the salt to keep it from toppling. Finally, fashion a pipe cleaner into a star and attach it to the tip of the tree.

Red-nosed Wreathdeer

Welcome visitors to your home with this friendly-faced reindeer. Start with a pinecone wreath (as we did) or modify this design for an evergreen wreath.

MATERIALS

- 10-inch square of corrugated cardboard
- Pinecone wreath with a 7-inch opening
- Adult-size brown knit ski cap
- Pair of brown gloves
- Fiberfill stuffing
- Low-temperature glue gun
- Cloth-covered floral wire
- 1 red pom-pom (2 inches wide)
- 2 white pom-poms (each 2 inches wide)
- Two ½-inch circles of black felt
- Small piece of brown craft foam
- 1 yard of wide ribbon tied into a bow

Lay down the cardboard with the wreath centered on top of it. Trace around the inside hole with a pen, then remove the wreath and draw a second circle about 1 inch larger than the first. Cut along the line for the larger circle.

Stuff the hat and gloves with fiberfill. Place the cardboard circle in the hat opening and glue about an inch of the hat material to it, as shown. Let dry. Carefully push the hat through the wreath until the cardboard back is flush against the back of the wreath. To hold in place, crisscross two pieces of floral wire across the back of the wreath and attach to the wreath to create a cross support.

If your wreath has a built-in hanger, make sure that it's at the top, then glue the red pom-pom nose and white pom-pom eyes onto the hat. Add a black felt circle to each eye.

Cut ears out of brown craft foam. (Ours are 4½ inches tall.) Wire the ears in place (just push floral wire through the foam and wrap around the wreath).

For each antler, cut three 18-inch pieces of floral wire. Fold down the top

inch of each wire and insert into the glove opening and up to the tops of three fingers. Twist the three wires together at the bottom of the glove and use to attach the antler to the wreath frame, as shown.

Use floral wire or a pipe cleaner to attach the bow (and bells, if you like) to the bottom of the wreath. Attach a wire loop at the back of the wreath to hang.

Peppermint Post

Sweeten your street during the holidays by decorating your mailbox with this mighty mint.

MATERIALS

- 3 Styrofoam disks 1 inch thick and 10 inches in diameter
- Tacky glue
- 6 feet of 2 3/4-inch-wide red metallic ribbon
- Straight pins
- Clear cellophane
- Twist ties
- Wire or twine

Stack and glue together the three Styrofoam disks. Cut the ribbon into six 12-inch lengths, trimming both ends of each piece into points. One at a time, glue the red stripes onto the Styrofoam. Start with one pointed end positioned near the center of the three-ply disk, then wrap the ribbon over the edge of the Styrofoam and glue the other end in place on the opposite side. Use straight pins to help hold the ends of the ribbons in place, then remove them once the glue has dried. Leave approximately 2½ inches between the ribbons. When all of the red stripes are in place, wrap the giant candy in a 30-inch square piece of the cellophane, scrunching the ends together and securing them with twist ties. Attach the finished decoration to your mailbox with wire or twine.

All-Pinecone Skier

Sometimes, the best holiday decorations capture your family's hobbies and personal passions. Here's an ornament that honors the ski buff in your family. The sporty decorations are made out of materials you should already have at home — Popsicle stick skis, toothpick ski poles, and a ski hat made out of an old glove.

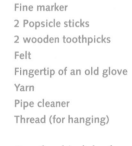

MATERIALS

- Hot glue gun
- Small wooden bead
- Small pinecone
- Fine marker
- 2 Popsicle sticks
- 2 wooden toothpicks
- Felt
- Fingertip of an old glove
- Yarn
- Pipe cleaner
- Thread (for hanging)

For the skier's body, use a hot glue gun to attach the wooden bead to the top of the small pinecone. Draw a face on the bead, if you wish. Then glue two Popsicle stick skis to the bottom and two wooden toothpicks to the sides for ski poles. A long, narrow piece of felt becomes a scarf to tie around the neck.

Cut a fingertip off an old glove for a knit cap. Or, add yarn hair and shape a pipe cleaner into a pair of earmuffs. Finally, tie a thread around the top of the cone and make a loop for hanging.

My Little Angel

Break out those leftover school photos and cast your child as an angel this Christmas with these adorable clip-on ornaments.

MATERIALS
- 6-inch paper doily
- Spring-action clothespin
- Glue
- Photo
- Gold pipe cleaner
- Gold foil paper

Fold the doily in half and then half again, to form a cone shape. Point the clothespin closed-side down. Glue the doily onto the top prong, forming the angel's dress. Cut a head out of a photo, then glue it onto the point of the doily. Wrap one end of the pipe cleaner around the bottom prong of the clothespin, shape into a halo, and trim.

Cut the gold foil paper to resemble wings and glue onto the back of the clothespin's top prong. Clip the clothespin mouth beneath the angel's skirt to the branches of your tree.

✳ EASY ORNAMENT

Beaded Beauties

Sometimes a simple idea, like shaping strands of beads into ornaments, is all it takes to check off most of the people on your child's gift list. The ones shown here are made with plastic beads that reflect light when you hang them on a Christmas tree or in front of a sunny window.

MATERIALS
- Pipe cleaners
- Transparent craft beads
  (5- to 10-millimeter diameters)

Bend an end of a pipe cleaner into a 90-degree angle. Have your child thread on beads from the opposite end, stopping a half inch from the tip. Then twist together the two ends, and the strand is ready to shape into a star, a candy cane, or another festive object. If he needs a longer strand to work with, twist together the ends of two pipe cleaners. Or, suggest he attach short beaded lengths to add a striker to a bell or holly berries to a wreath, for example.

Star of David Mobile

As part of a bi-religious family, *FamilyFun* contributing editor Jodi Picoult's kids each have their favorite Hanukkah traditions along with their Christmas ones. For her son Jake, "the extremely cool thing is getting eight presents, one for each night of the holiday." Her son Kyle likes lighting the menorah. And her daughter, Sammy, loves getting elbow-deep in shredded potatoes when they make latkes. But everyone in the family jumped to participate when it came time to craft these six-pointed stars (the symbolic Star of David) to string in their windows.

MATERIALS
   Pipe cleaners
   String

For each star, you'll need two pipe cleaners. Fold each one into thirds to form a triangle. Hold one triangle in your left hand and the other triangle in your right hand so that the tops point toward each other (as shown). Now weave the top of A down through the center of B, and the top of B up through the center of A. Next, tuck the point of A under the base of B, and slip the point of B over the base of A. Use this method to make as many stars as you like. Then tie them together with string and hang.

Remember the Animals

Legend has it that on Christmas Eve, all animals are granted the ability to speak until daybreak. While the following tradition doesn't guarantee you a verbal thank-you from the neighborhood wildlife, it's a nice way to treat your animal friends when food is scarce.

MATERIALS

- Large outdoor pine tree
- Pinecones rolled in peanut butter and birdseed
- Popcorn-and-peanut garlands
- Orange and apple slices suspended from pipe cleaners
- Carrots tied with twine

Providing treats for the animals need not be elaborate. Putting out birdseed or peanut butter sandwiches for the squirrels will suffice. But for a truly lovely twist, you can take a cue from the Waterman family of St. Charles, Missouri. Inspired by Eve Bunting's book *Night Tree*, the Watermans get together each year with friends and family and trek into the woods to decorate a tree for the animals.

The evening begins at home, with the preparation of appropriate goodies: the pinecones, garland, and fruit treats suggested above. Once the feast is complete, the assembled throng bundles up and heads out into the night. Tree decking is followed by sharing hot chocolate, holiday cookies, and Christmas carols.

✷ EASY ORNAMENT
Snappy Soldiers

Dressed in red jackets and Tudor bonnets, these wooden soldiers are ready to stand sentry around the Christmas tree.

MATERIALS
- Old-fashioned clothespins
- Acrylic paint (white, black, red, brown, and gold)
- Red and black pom-poms
- White glue
- Gold thread
- Shoe box

Paint white or black trousers on each clothespin. Holding the clothespin by its rounded top, paint the portion from the upper edge of the split down to the tips. As you finish this step, pin the clothespins on the edge of the shoe box and let them dry.

Next, mix dabs of red, white, and brown paint to create a skin tone and use it to paint the soldiers' heads. Paint on red jackets, as shown. Again, let the paint dry.

Now paint on distinguishing details, such as gold buttons and buckles, black arm outlines and facial features, and white gloves. Glue a red or black pom-pom onto the heads to create the soldiers' bonnets. Loop a length of gold thread around each clothespin below the soldier's head to use as a hanger.

✷ TABLETOP DECORATION
Trinket Tree

Made from household trinkets and doodads, this festive gilded tree makes a great conversation piece for holiday guests. Or, set it on your child's nightstand or dresser, and it's sure to inspire sweet dreams of Christmas morning.

MATERIALS
- Hard plastic cereal bowl, 5 inches in diameter
- Tacky glue
- Corrugated cardboard circle, 8 inches in diameter
- Styrofoam cone, 12 inches tall
- Roll of twine (optional)
- Lots of trinkets and tiny toys
- Low-temperature hot glue gun
- Toothpick
- Gold spray paint

Use tacky glue to join the bottom of the bowl to the center of the cardboard circle. Once the glue dries, invert the bowl and glue the base of the foam cone atop the other side of the cardboard. Again, let the glue dry.

For a wider tree, wrap twine repeatedly around the cone until you've achieved the desired width. Then glue the loose twine ends in place. For a tall, slim tree, go right to the next step.

Have your child glue on the trinkets one at a time. Start with larger ones arranged around the base and build upward using increasingly smaller objects. Some items, especially weightier ones, may need to be hot-glued in place (a parent's job), but many should hold well with the tacky glue, which is more child-friendly.

For a treetop ornament, choose one with a hollow portion, such as a bell, whistle, or seashell. Then insert one end of the toothpick into the top of the cone and set the tree topper over the protruding end.

Place the adorned tree on newspaper in a well-ventilated area and apply several coats of gold spray paint (another job for adults only). Allow the paint to dry completely.

The Story of the Christmas Tree

The true origin of the Christmas tree may be lost to history, but there are a few credible theories kicking around. The most prevalent credits Martin Luther, the German leader of the 16th-century Protestant movement. While out late one evening, Luther looked up through the top branches of pine trees into the night sky, which was filled with stars. When he arrived home, he tried in vain to explain to his family the beautiful image he had just seen. To recreate it, he brought in a cut fir tree and decorated it with lighted candles.

Creative Sugar Cookies, page 45

CHAPTER TWO

Holiday Foods We Love

FOR MANY OF US, the sweetest part of the holiday season is baking with our children. We put on holiday music, pull out the measuring cups and cookie sheets, and spend a few hours together in the kitchen mixing up cookie dough and assembling holiday treats. This annual baking session has become a family tradition — something we look forward to every December.

In this chapter, you'll find dozens of creative recipes to add to your family's repertoire. Each one is relatively easy to prepare and has steps that involve the kids in the cooking process. With our recipes and a few basic ingredients, it won't be long before you and your kids have baked up dozens of treats to bring to holiday parties, give as gifts, and, of course, leave for Santa on Christmas Eve.

Be prepared. At the beginning of the season, stock up on basic ingredients (flour, sugar, and butter) as well as holiday extras (red and green food coloring, creative cookie cutters, and colored sprinkles). That way, you won't have to make dozens of trips to the grocery store during the busiest time of the year.

Review cooking basics with your kids. Before inviting the kids into the kitchen, set up a workspace that's easy for them to reach (a countertop with stools or a low table with chairs) and clear it off so there's plenty of room in which to work. Have them wash their hands, tie back their hair, and put on aprons. Read through the recipe with them, then gather the ingredients and equipment needed. For best results, teach your kids to measure carefully and accurately.

Candy Express, page 42

Take shortcuts. To relieve some of the holiday pressure, prepare a few batches of cookie dough (try the sugar cookie dough on page 45 or the gingerbread dough on page 36) when you have spare time. Then wrap in sealable plastic bags and freeze. During the holiday rush, just defrost and proceed with the recipe. In a matter of minutes, you'll have freshly baked cookies, ready for your kids to decorate.

Share gifts from the kitchen. Instead of buying presents for teachers and friends, help your kids bake deliciously thoughtful gifts in the kitchen. Try holiday favorites, such as the Cinnamon Coffee Cake on page 47. For a quicker kitchen gift, assemble one of our no-bake treats, such as the Chocolate Granola Clusters on page 53. And don't forget to include a recipe card.

Cinnamon Roll Wreath

On a December afternoon, invite your kids into the kitchen to help you knead this sweet yeast bread and roll it up with cinnamon and sugar.

INGREDIENTS

Dough:
- $1/2$ cup butter
- $2/3$ cup milk
- $1/3$ cup water
- $1/4$ ounce package active dry yeast
- $1/2$ cup sugar
- 1 teaspoon salt
- 2 eggs, beaten
- 4 to 5 cups all purpose flour

Filling:
- 1 cup brown sugar
- 2 tablespoons cinnamon
- 4 tablespoons softened butter
- 1 cup walnuts (optional)
- 1 cup raisins

Icing:
- 1 cup confectioners' sugar
- 2 to 3 tablespoons milk

In a medium-size saucepan, melt $1/2$ cup of butter over low heat. Add the milk and water and heat until just warm (about 100°). Pour the liquid into a large bowl and add the yeast. Stir to dissolve. Mix in the sugar, salt, and beaten eggs. Next, add the flour, 1 cup at a time,

mixing well after each addition until the dough forms a ball.

Turn out the dough onto a lightly floured surface and knead for about

5 minutes (the dough should be sticky; just add enough flour to make it workable). Place the dough in a buttered bowl, cover, and let rise in a warm, draft-free place for about 3 hours or until doubled in bulk.

Meanwhile, mix the brown sugar and cinnamon in a small bowl. Once the dough has risen, punch it down and divide it in half. Roll one half into a large rectangle (about 6 by 20 inches). Spread evenly with half the softened butter and sprinkle with half the filling mixture and, if desired, half the walnuts and raisins.

Beginning at the long end, roll up the dough jelly-roll style. Pinch the edges to seal and shape into a wreath. Repeat with the remaining dough. Place both wreaths on a buttered cookie sheet and slice each round, three fourths of the way down, into eighths. Cover and let rise for 1 hour.

Heat the oven to 350°. Bake for 30 minutes or until light brown. While the wreaths cool, mix up the icing. In a small bowl, stir the confectioners' sugar with the milk. Drizzle the icing over the wreaths.

Next, cut out a circle of cardboard and cover with foil. Place the wreath on the tray, wrap in colored plastic, tie with a red bow, and attach a handmade gift card. Present the wreaths to neighbors, teachers, and friends, but be sure to save one for your own family's holiday breakfast. Makes 2.

HOT CIDER SACHET

Here's a spicy holiday gift that kids can craft in the kitchen with a little help from you. Ask your child to cut an 8-inch square out of a double layer of cheesecloth and lay it flat. Mound 15 allspice berries, 2 teaspoons of whole cloves, and 2 cinnamon sticks, broken into pieces, in the center. To form the sachet, gather up the sides of the cheesecloth and tie them together

with cooking twine. Trim off any extra fabric.

To make an accompanying gift tag, fold an index card in half, punch a hole in the upper left corner, and personalize the front with a drawing (perhaps a mug or an apple tree). On the inside, have your child write the following directions: "Pour $1/2$ gallon cider into a large pot. Drop in sachet. Bring to a boil, reduce the heat, and simmer for 20 minutes. Serve warm in mugs." Lastly, thread a ribbon through the hole in the card and tie it around the sachet.

Saint Lucia's Bread

On December 13th, Saint Lucia Day, your family can pay homage to the fourth-century saint remembered for her hospitality. This festive bread is inspired by the candle-covered crown she is said to have worn to light her way as she brought food to the poor.

INGREDIENTS

	Cinnamon Roll Wreath dough (at left)
2¹/₂	cups confectioners' sugar
2¹/₂	to 3¹/₂ tablespoons orange juice
¹/₃	cup dried cranberries

Follow the directions for making the dough for the Cinnamon Roll Wreath. Once it has risen, punch it down and divide it into 3 equal parts. Roll each part into a 30-inch rope and braid the ropes together. Transfer the braid to a buttered baking sheet, pinch together the ends to form a circle, and let it rise until it has again doubled in size, about 1 to 2 hours. Bake at 350° for 30 minutes or until light brown.

For the glaze, stir together the confectioners' sugar and orange juice in a medium bowl until smooth. Drizzle the glaze mix over the bread, then garnish with the cranberries. Finally, add candles, if you'd like. Serves 12.

Jolly Snowman Bread

Help your kids shape this classic white bread dough into smiley snowmen.

INGREDIENTS

5¹/₂	cups all-purpose flour
2	tablespoons brown sugar
2	teaspoons salt
¹/₂	cup warm water (100°)
¹/₄	ounce package active dry yeast
	Pinch of sugar
1¹/₂	cups warm milk
4	tablespoons softened butter
	Raisins, dried apricots, and gumdrops

In a large bowl, combine the flour, brown sugar, and salt. Set aside. Pour the warm water into a separate large bowl and sprinkle in the yeast and a pinch of sugar. Stir and let the mix sit for 5 minutes, until bubbles begin to appear. Stir in the warm milk, butter, and 2 cups of the dry ingredients. Stir in the remaining dry ingredients 1 cup at a time, mixing until the dough is stiff.

Turn the dough out onto a lightly floured countertop and knead for 5 to 10 minutes or until the dough becomes smooth and springs when touched. Butter a large mixing bowl, place the dough in the bowl, and cover it with a dish towel. Let it rise for 1½ hours or until doubled in bulk.

Punch down the dough. Divide it into 4 pieces (1 for each snowman). Cut off the top third of each piece and shape it into the snowman's head; shape the larger piece into a ball for the body. Place the 2 balls on a baking sheet and pinch them together. Repeat with the remaining 3 pieces of dough until you have 4 snowmen. Cover and let them rise for 30 to 45 minutes.

Heat the oven to 350°. Brush the snowmen with milk and adorn with raisin eyes, a dried apricot nose, and gumdrop buttons. Cover the fruit and gumdrops with small pieces of aluminum foil so they won't burn, then bake for 30 minutes or until golden brown. Cool on racks. To present, wrap in plastic and tie a ribbon around each snowman's neck for a scarf. Makes 4 snowmen.

Dancing Ginger People

After rolling and cutting this sturdy cookie dough, your kids can bend the gingerbread figures' arms or legs — and make a gang of gingerbread people dance on the tree.

INGREDIENTS

$4^1/_2$ cups all-purpose flour
1   teaspoon baking soda
1   tablespoon ground cinnamon
1   teaspoon ground ginger
$^1/_2$ cup butter, at room temperature
$^3/_4$ cup brown sugar
2   eggs
$^3/_4$ cup molasses
     Best-Ever Cookie Frosting
       (see page 44)
     Candies, sprinkles, and colored
       sugar
     Ribbon

In a mixing bowl, stir together the flour, baking soda, cinnamon, and ginger. In a separate large bowl, cream the butter and brown sugar with an electric mixer. Beat in the eggs one at a time, then beat in the molasses.

Gradually add the dry ingredients, blending until the flour is thoroughly mixed in. Divide the dough in half, wrap in plastic, and chill for 2 hours.

Heat the oven to 350° and lightly grease a baking sheet. On a floured surface, roll out one half of the dough to ¼-inch thickness. Cut out gingerbread people with a cookie cutter. Use a spatula to transfer them to the baking sheet and, with the end of a chopstick, poke a hole in the top of each cookie for hanging. To make the people dance, carefully bend their arms and legs before baking.

Bake the cookies for 10 to 12 minutes or until brown. Repoke the hole if necessary. Cool slightly, then transfer to a wire rack.

Decorate with frosting and candies. Pipe or spread on frosting shirts and shoes, then sprinkle with colored sugar. Make funny faces with gumdrops, shoestring licorice, and M&M's Minis. Lastly, thread a ribbon through the hole in each gingerbread person and hang on the tree. Makes about 24 cookies.

Christmas Eve Cookies

"Ever since I can remember, I have baked gingerbread cookies on Christmas Eve afternoon. When I was a child, my mom helped me with this ritual, as we mixed up the dough, rolled it out, and cut out gingerbread people with a red plastic cookie cutter. My sisters and I would then squirt on icing and attach Red Hot candies. As an adult, I continue to bake gingerbread cookies every Christmas Eve, still using the same cookie cutter, now slightly cracked, that my family has used for the past 25 or 30 years."

— Emily B. Todd
Northampton, Massachusetts

GINGERBREAD HOUSE COOKIES

Don't have time to build a complete gingerbread house? Bake and decorate these 2-D cottages. Follow the gingerbread cookie dough recipe at left. While it chills, design homemade cookie templates out of poster board. For best results, choose a fairly simple design, such as a 3-inch square house with a triangular roof. Then carefully cut out the shape. Lay the template on the rolled out dough and trace around it with a sharp knife (parents and older kids only). Bake according to the recipe directions. Once the houses have cooled, use decorators' frosting to "glue" candies — try a Necco wafer roof, peppermint disk windows, and licorice-bordered doors.

Old-fashioned Gingerbread

This moist gingerbread cake, spiced with ginger, cinnamon, and nutmeg, tastes just right with a tall glass of cold milk.

INGREDIENTS

2¹/₂ cups all-purpose flour
1 tablespoon ground ginger
1 teaspoon cinnamon
¹/₄ teaspoon nutmeg
1 teaspoon baking powder
¹/₂ teaspoon baking soda
¹/₂ teaspoon salt
¹/₂ cup butter
³/₄ cup molasses
¹/₃ cup brown sugar
2 eggs
1 cup milk
Whipped cream or applesauce

Heat the oven to 350°. Butter a 9-inch square baking pan. Next, flour the pan: place a tablespoon of flour in the buttered pan and turn the pan back and forth until the flour completely coats the surface.

To mix the gingerbread batter, first sift the flour, ginger, cinnamon, nutmeg, baking powder, baking soda, and salt into a medium-size bowl. Set aside.

In a microwave, melt the butter (about 40 seconds on high). In a large mixing bowl, stir the melted butter, molasses, and brown sugar. Crack the eggs into a separate small bowl, whisk, and then mix into the butter mixture. Alternately add the flour mixture and milk to the butter-egg mixture, beginning and ending with the flour. Pour the mixture into the prepared baking pan and bake for 35 minutes or until a knife inserted in the middle of the cake comes out clean. Let the cake cool in the pan. Slice into 9 squares. Top each piece with a dollop of whipped cream or applesauce. Serves 9.

✳ GIFT FROM THE KITCHEN

Gingerbread Family Kit

This kit of baked gingerbread men, decorators' frosting, and candies will give a family all the pleasures of cookie decorating without the mess of baking.

KIT SUPPLIES

Baked gingerbread men (see recipe at left)

White decorators' frosting, M&M's Minis, cinnamon Red Hots, tissue paper, plastic containers, shoestring licorice

To assemble a kit, line a 9-inch square plastic container with tissue paper, and add about 4 undecorated cookies, candies for decorating the cookies, and a tube of frosting. Have your child design a label to affix to the lid that says "Gingerbread Family Kit." One batch of cookies makes 4 to 5 kits.

Snowman Cake

This friendly chocolate cake, from *FamilyFun* contributor Joan Cirillo, makes a fun party centerpiece.

INGREDIENTS

- 1³/₄ cups cake flour
- ¹/₂ cup Dutch-processed cocoa
- 1¹/₄ teaspoons baking powder
- ¹/₂ teaspoon baking soda
- ¹/₂ teaspoon salt
- ¹/₂ cup butter, softened
- 1¹/₂ cups sugar
- 3 large eggs
- 1 teaspoon vanilla extract
- 1 cup milk
- 1¹/₂ cups vanilla frosting
- Shredded coconut (optional)
- Candy decorations

Heat the oven to 325°. Grease and flour two ovenproof glass bowls, one slightly larger than the other (we used one 6-inch diameter and one 7-inch). Mix the flour, cocoa, baking powder, baking soda, and salt into a large mixing bowl. In a separate large bowl, cream the butter with the sugar until light and fluffy. Add the eggs, one at a time, mixing well after each addition. Mix in the vanilla extract. Alternately add the flour mixture and the milk to the batter in thirds, mixing well after each addition.

Fill the bowls about two thirds full. Bake the smaller cake for about 50 minutes and the larger cake for about 65 minutes. When done, a toothpick inserted in the center will come out clean. Cool in the bowls for 10 minutes. Then invert onto a large, rectangular platter so the cakes resemble a snowman. Cool completely.

Frost the cakes, then sprinkle with shredded coconut. Add licorice drop eyes, an orange gumdrop nose, a shoestring licorice smile, fruit leather scarf, starlight mints topped with gumdrops, and chocolate licorice arms. Serves 10.

Claus Cake

With the tip of his red cap tucked around his fuzzy white chin, this miniature Santa cake is both adorable and delicious. A plateful will be the hit of any Christmas party.

INGREDIENTS

Cupcake
White and red icing
Mini marshmallow
Shredded coconut
Blue and pink gel icing
Red candy

Frost the cupcake with a layer of white icing. Add the red frosting hat, curving it around the side of Santa's face, and a marshmallow pom-pom. Sprinkle on a ring of coconut to make Santa's beard and hair. Draw on his eyes and cheeks with gel icing, then top it all off with a red candy nose.

HOLLY CUPCAKES

'Tis the season when you're sure to need a special dessert to bring to a Christmas party or school bake sale. With this easy decorating tip, you and your kids can turn a batch of homemade or store-bought cupcakes into a festive treat.

First, frost the cupcakes with snowy white icing and top with grated coconut. Then use a rolling pin to flatten green gumdrops on a piece of waxed paper sprinkled with sugar. Use an aspic cutter or a butter knife to cut out holly leaf shapes. Arrange 2 or 3 leaves and a few red candy "berries" on top of each cupcake, pressing them into the frosting just enough to hold them in place.

Cupcake Menorah

Menorahs, the nine-candled lamps that Jews light on the eight nights of Hanukkah, have long been up for grabs, artistically. They are made of clay, silver, wood, glass — just about any material the artist's imagination can conceive. So *FamilyFun* editor Dawn Chipman asked herself, what could be more kid-friendly than a cupcake menorah to enjoy at a party on the last day of Hanukkah?

INGREDIENTS

8   baked mini cupcakes
1   baked regular size cupcake
    Frosting and blue colored sugar
    Hanukkah or birthday candles

Frost the cupcakes and sprinkle with the blue sugar. To assemble the menorah, place the cupcakes on a platter or board. Set the large frosted cupcake in the middle with four mini cupcakes at each side. Insert a Hanukkah or birthday candle into each cupcake, with a shammes, or leader candle, in the larger cupcake. (To collect wax drips, use plastic candleholders. Alternatively, use chocolate-dipped pretzel stick "candles," adding one each day.) Light your menorah in the traditional manner. Light the shammes in the large cupcake. Let your kids use the lit shammes to light the other candles, left to right, until the room gleams with candlelight. Then dig into this party treat. (Depending on the number of guests at your party, you might need to make more than one menorah.)

SUGARED NUTS

These cinnamony nuts make a sweet gift for a favorite teacher or neighbor. You may want to make a double batch so there'll be plenty for your kitchen helpers to nibble on too.

Heat the oven to 300°. In a mixing bowl, stir together $1/2$ cup of sugar, 1 teaspoon of cinnamon, $1/2$ teaspoon of nutmeg, and $1/8$ teaspoon of salt. In a separate bowl, gently mix 1 egg white and 1 tablespoon of water and then stir in 2 cups of almonds and pecans.

Next, pour the sugar mixture over the nuts and stir until evenly coated. Spread the nuts on a waxed-paper-lined baking sheet. Bake for 30 minutes. Let cool for a few minutes before removing the nuts from the sheet.

✳ PARTY FOOD
Wrap 'n' Stack Tree

Can't decide what to bring to a tree-trimming party? Bring this edible tree. Made from mini sandwiches and trimmed with colorful vegetables, it can serve as a healthy alternative to the usual array of holiday sweets.

INGREDIENTS

- 1 **16-ounce can whole-berry cranberry sauce**
- 4 **large (9- or 10-inch) spinach-flour tortillas or flat bread Mayonnaise**
- $3/4$ **pound thinly sliced Monterey Jack or American cheese**
- $3/4$ **pound thinly sliced smoked turkey**
- $1/2$ **head green-leaf lettuce Toothpicks Red and yellow bell peppers and cocktail onions, for garnish**

Spoon the cranberry sauce into a food processor and pulse it briefly. Then lay the tortillas or flat bread on a flat working surface and lightly spread them with mayonnaise (a rubber spatula comes in handy for this). Now your kids can top each tortilla with a layer each of cheese and turkey. **Tip:** When stacking ingredients, leave an inch margin along the top of the tortilla. Roll the bread toward that edge to keep the filling from falling out.

Spread cranberry sauce on the turkey layers and cover them with lettuce. Snugly roll up the sandwiches, ending with the loose edges underneath. With a serrated knife, cut each roll-up into 1¼-inch-wide pinwheels and insert a toothpick to hold each one together.

On a serving platter, arrange the pinwheels in rows to create a Christmas tree. Garnish with bell pepper star "ornaments" (cut out with a small cookie cutter) and cocktail onion "lights." Serves about 12.

EGGS-CELLENT NOG

Our alcohol-free version of this holiday party staple is cooked (so it's safe) and then chilled quickly with a secret ingredient.

Whisk 6 egg yolks, 1/2 cup of sugar, and 1/2 teaspoon of ground nutmeg in a large bowl. In a medium saucepan over medium heat, heat 2 cups of milk until it steams. Pour some of the hot milk over the egg mixture and whisk (this keeps the eggs from scrambling), then scrape this egg mixture into the saucepan with the rest of the milk. Cook over medium-low heat, whisking constantly, until it thickens a bit, about 10 minutes (or 165° to 175°). Remove from the heat and stir in 1 cup of half and half and 1 tablespoon of vanilla extract. Pour through a strainer into a clean bowl. Add 1 pint of superpremium vanilla ice cream, and stir until melted. Chill at least 1 hour, then stir before serving. Garnish with nutmeg. Serves 12.

O Christmas Treat

Trimmed with bell pepper ornaments and feta snowflakes, this spinach pizza makes a savory holiday appetizer.

INGREDIENTS

- 1 package frozen, chopped spinach
- Yellow, red, and orange bell peppers
- Olive oil
- Cornmeal
- Pizza dough for one 12-inch round pie (homemade or store-bought)
- 1 cup tomato sauce
- 1/4 to 1/3 cup grated Romano cheese
- Feta cheese

Heat the oven to 450°. Cook the spinach, drain, and press it to squeeze out excess liquid. Set aside.

Use tiny cookie cutters to shape circles and stars from the peppers. Set aside.

Coat a 12-inch pizza pan with olive oil, then sprinkle on the cornmeal. Roll the dough into a circle and place on the pan, pushing the edges to the rim.

Spread the tomato sauce on the dough and sprinkle on the grated Romano cheese. Top with the chopped spinach and then drizzle olive oil over the spinach. Sprinkle the crumbled feta over the spinach and arrange the pepper circles.

Bake for about 20 minutes, or until the bottom of the crust is browned. Cut the pizza into triangular slices and then trim the crust to form a trunk. Finally, top each slice with a yellow star. Makes one 12-inch pizza.

MULTICULTURAL POTLUCK

If you want to host a holiday gathering, but feel it will be too much work, try this simple potluck with an international twist. Ask guests to bring a dish they enjoy during their holiday celebration that reflects their family's heritage. Descendants of Spain may bring red cabbage, while Irish families bake soda bread and Icelandic friends contribute smoked salmon.

Once you know what nations will be represented, your kids can get busy making decorations that celebrate them. With paper and crayons, have them make flags (check a world atlas for pictures of the world's flags). Next, tape the flags to straws. Then, for colorful centerpieces, stick the straw flagpoles into small blocks of Styrofoam covered with metallic wrapping paper.

To dine cafe-style, set the food and dishes out in one room and prepare another room with several card tables and chairs. Cover each table with a white paper tablecloth, and crisscross strands of blue and red crepe paper over the center, topping it with one of your flag centerpieces. On each table, you could provide the words to a simple grace your guests can say together.

For quick cleanup, use paper plates and have each family bring home their leftovers.

Red-nosed Reindeer Lollipop

With its lollipop head, pipe cleaner antlers, and googly eyes, this treat is part craft project, part holiday sweet. Kids can easily make a whole herd for classmates and teachers.

MATERIALS

- Large round lollipop
- Plastic wrap
- Clear and double-sided tape
- Brown pipe cleaner
- Tiny bell
- Red ribbon
- Self-adhesive googly eyes
- Red pom-pom

Unwrap the lollipop and cover it again with plastic wrap. Secure it at the base with clear tape. Bend the pipe cleaner in half around the base of the pop and shape the ends into antlers (as shown below). Thread the bell onto a 10-inch length of red ribbon and tie it around the reindeer's neck. Stick on the googly eyes and attach the pom-pom nose with double-sided tape.

★ QUICK TREAT

CANDY EXPRESS

Looking for a way to sweeten the wait for Santa's sleigh? Cut off and discard the top of a small square cracker or tissue box. Trim the cut edge of the box bottom so that it resembles a sleigh. Cut holes in the lower corners of the sleigh and insert candy cane "runners." Fill the sleigh with candy for all to enjoy.

✳ QUICK TREAT

Peppermint Tree

With green mint boughs and sour ball lights, this tabletop tree is a treat to decorate for kids — and for holiday guests, who can harvest goodies from its branches.

MATERIALS

- Double-sided foam tape
- 9- by 4-inch Styrofoam cones (sold in most craft stores)
- Three 10-ounce bags of individually wrapped green striped mints
- Small bag of individually wrapped multicolored sour balls or jawbreakers
- Yellow paper
- Yellow lollipop
- Decorative candle stand

Apply strips of double-sided foam tape to the Styrofoam cone, as shown below at left, until virtually the entire surface is covered. Now your child can attach the wrapped mints to the exposed tape, starting with one row around the bottom and working his way up. For the best coverage and color, he should stick each mint to the tree by the rounded edge rather than with the flat surface facing out. Encourage him to mix in a few multicolored sour ball or jawbreaker lights as he goes.

For a tree topper, cut a star out of the yellow paper, tape the lollipop to it, and then push the lollipop stick straight down into the cone. Finally, set the tree on the decorative candle stand.

✳ GIFT FROM THE KITCHEN

MINT-CHOCOLATE BARK

Your holiday guests won't be able to resist this delectable combination of sweet chocolate and crunchy mint. Don't be surprised if the batch disappears before your eyes!

Line a 13- by 9-inch baking pan with aluminum foil and set it aside. Break 12 ounces of white chocolate, such as Ghirardelli, into pieces and melt them in a double boiler or microwave according to the package directions. Remove the pan from the heat and stir in $1/3$ cup of crushed candy cane pieces. Pour the mixture onto the foil-lined pan, spreading it to within $1/2$ inch of the edges. Melt 2 tablespoons of semisweet chocolate chips and drizzle them over the white chocolate mixture. Sprinkle on extra crushed candy pieces.

Place the bark in the refrigerator and chill until firm, about 15 minutes. Then break or cut into pieces. Serve at room temperature.

✳ GIFT FROM THE KITCHEN

Peanut Brittle

This near instant peanut candy is a favorite recipe of *FamilyFun* editor Jon Adolph's family. (Note: When the syrup comes out of the microwave, it is very hot. Pouring it is a parent's job.)

INGREDIENTS

- 1 cup sugar
- $1/2$ cup light corn syrup
- 1 cup dry-roasted peanuts
- $1/8$ teaspoon salt
- 1 teaspoon butter or margarine
- 1 teaspoon vanilla extract
- 1 teaspoon baking soda

In a 1½-quart microwave-safe bowl, stir together the sugar, syrup, peanuts, and salt, mixing well. Microwave on high for 6½ minutes. (Times will vary depending on microwave wattage. We based these times on an 850-watt oven.) Carefully swirl the butter or margarine and vanilla extract into the mixture; don't stir. Microwave for another 30 seconds. The peanuts should be light brown, the syrup will have darkened slightly, and the mixture will be very hot (300° on a candy thermometer). Add the baking soda and gently stir the mixture until it's light and foamy. Pour it onto a lightly buttered cookie sheet. Let the brittle cool for 30 minutes to 1 hour, then break it into small pieces. Makes 2 pounds.

Jolly Jelly Thumbprints

With these jelly-filled cookies, even very young chefs can make their mark on cookie dough. For other filling options, try pressing a few chocolate chips, M&M's, or a chocolate kiss into the just-baked cookies.

INGREDIENTS

- 1 cup (2 sticks) unsalted butter, softened
- 1/2 cup firmly packed brown sugar
- 1 large egg
- 1 teaspoon vanilla extract
- 3 cups all-purpose flour
- 1/2 teaspoon salt
- Granulated sugar (for rolling cookies)
- About 1/2 cup jelly or preserves

In a large mixing bowl, using a wooden spoon, cream the butter and brown sugar together until smooth. Stir in the egg and vanilla extract until combined. Gradually stir in the flour and salt. Cover the dough and refrigerate it for at least 1 to 2 hours or until the dough is firm enough to roll into balls.

Heat the oven to 350°. Form scant tablespoonfuls of the dough into 1-inch balls. Roll the balls in a bowl of granulated sugar. Place the balls on an ungreased baking sheet, leaving 2 inches between them. Using your thumb, your knuckle, or the end of a wooden spoon, press an indentation into the center of each cookie. If the cookie cracks, press the crack together to make it smooth. Fill the center of each cookie with about 1/2 teaspoon of jelly. Bake for 10 to 12 minutes or until lightly browned.

Cool on the baking sheets for about 2 minutes, then transfer to a wire rack to cool completely. Repeat until all the dough is used. These cookies can be stored in an airtight container at room temperature for 1 week. Makes 4 dozen.

✳ QUICK TREAT
BEST-EVER COOKIE FROSTING

Decorate the Creative Sugar Cookies at right with this buttercream frosting. In a large bowl, using an electric mixer, beat 2 cups of sifted confectioners' sugar, 1/4 cup of unsalted softened butter, and 1/2 teaspoon of vanilla extract, until it reaches a spreading consistency. Add more sugar or 1 to 2 tablespoons of milk, if necessary, to achieve the right texture. Stir in food coloring. Spread the frosting onto the cookies or pipe it through a pastry bag fitted with a decorators' tip (or a sealable plastic bag with a snip cut out of one corner). Makes about 1 cup.

Creative Sugar Cookies

This easy-to-make cookie dough can be rolled and cut into festive shapes, then baked and decorated to look like windows, trees, and Santas.

INGREDIENTS

- 1/2 cup unsalted butter, softened
- 3 tablespoons vegetable shortening
- 3/4 cup sugar
- 1 large egg
- 1 teaspoon vanilla extract
- 1 3/4 cups all-purpose flour
- 1 teaspoon baking powder
- 1/4 teaspoon salt
- Best-Ever Cookie Frosting (see recipe at left)
- Assorted candies for decorating

Using an electric mixer, cream the butter and shortening. Gradually add the sugar, beating until fluffy. Beat in the egg and the vanilla extract.

Sift the flour, baking powder, and salt into a separate bowl. Using a wooden spoon, stir the dry mixture into the creamed ingredients, about a third at a time. Divide the dough in half and pat it into two disks. Wrap in plastic and refrigerate for 2 to 4 hours, until firm.

Heat the oven to 350°. Lightly grease two baking sheets. Working between two pieces of waxed paper, roll out one dough disk at a time until it is 1/8 to 1/4 inch thick. Remove the top sheet and cut out the cookies with cookie cutters or a knife (see below for suggestions).

Place the cookies on the prepared baking sheet. Bake for 8 to 12 minutes or until the cookie edges turn light brown. Cool on a wire rack, then decorate with icing and candies. Makes 12 to 20 cookies, depending on their size.

Christmas Tree Pops: Cut the cookie dough into 3 1/4-inch-tall triangles. Place on the prepared cookie sheets. Insert a craft stick three quarters of the way under each cookie. Bake according to recipe directions. Once cool, decorate with piped on icing and candy "lights."

Sugar Cookie Windows: Cut the cookie dough into rectangles (3 by 4 inches). With a chopstick, poke holes for hanging at the tops. Bake the cookies according to recipe directions. Frost, then add candy flower boxes and fruit leather curtains. Hang with a ribbon.

Kris Kringle Cookies: Cut out the cookie dough using a heart-shaped cookie cutter and bake according to recipe directions. Once cooled, turn each heart upside down and frost the rounded parts with white icing.

Then top with shredded coconut to create Santa's beard. Use red decorating gel to turn the point of the heart into Santa's hat and add more coconut for the trim. Add mini chocolate chip eyes and a red gel nose.

Cookie Carolers: Cut out rounds of cookie dough. Using a chopstick, poke a hole in the center of each cookie and wiggle it to make a wide open mouth. Bake according to recipe directions. Repoke the holes. Once cooled, use icing to pipe on hair, eyes, and freckles.

Perfect Pancake Mix

Preparing this whole-grain pancake mix will take you and your child merely minutes, but the recipient will enjoy leisurely breakfasts for weeks.

INGREDIENTS

5	cups all-purpose flour
$1^1/_2$	cups whole wheat flour
1	cup cornmeal
$^1/_3$	cup sugar
2	tablespoons plus 2 teaspoons baking powder
2	teaspoons salt

Measure the all-purpose flour, whole wheat flour, cornmeal, sugar, baking powder, and salt into the bowl of a large food processor. Process for 15 to 30 seconds or until thoroughly mixed. (Alternatively, stir the ingredients together in a bowl.) Spoon the mix into a 2-quart jar.

Affix a label on the front of the jar that says "Pancake Mix." Affix a second label on the back of the jar with the pancake directions: "Stir 1½ cups of pancake mix, 2 eggs, and 1¼ cups of milk in a mixing bowl until smooth. Melt 1 tablespoon of butter in a large frying pan over medium heat. Cook the pancakes for 2 to 3 minutes on each side. Enjoy with maple syrup. Serves 4." To present the gift, tie a bow around the jar. Makes 1 mix.

Lemon Poppy Seed Gift Loaf

Give your friends this scrumptious loaf of holiday cheer for Christmas. Dress it in plastic wrap tied with a bow or, for an extra-special touch, present it in a new loaf pan (to ensure the right fit, bake the loaf in the new pan and wash it after baking).

INGREDIENTS

Loaf:

$^1/_2$	cup softened butter
1	cup sugar
2	eggs
1	teaspoon grated lemon peel
$1^1/_2$	cups all-purpose flour
1	teaspoon baking powder
$^1/_2$	teaspoon salt
$^1/_3$	cup milk
2	tablespoons poppy seeds

Glaze:

	Juice of 1 lemon
$^1/_2$	cup confectioners' sugar

Heat the oven to 350°. Grease a 9-by 5-inch loaf pan. In a mixing bowl, beat the butter and sugar. Beat in the remaining ingredients in the order listed. Pour the mix into the pan and bake for 55 minutes or until a toothpick inserted into the center comes out clean. Let the loaf cool for 15 minutes, then transfer it to a cooling rack. Meanwhile, mix together the glaze ingredients. Prick the loaf with a fork and pour the glaze over the top. Makes 1 loaf.

Jelly Roll

You can use any seedless jam to fill this jammin' good jelly roll.

INGREDIENTS

$1/2$	cup cake or all-purpose flour
3	tablespoons cornstarch
$1/2$	teaspoon baking powder
$1/4$	teaspoon salt
5	large eggs
$1/2$	cup sugar
1	teaspoon vanilla extract
	Confectioners' sugar
$3/4$	cup fruit preserves or seedless jam

Heat the oven to 350°. Grease a 15-by 10-inch jelly roll pan, then line it with waxed paper or parchment. Butter the paper and dust it with flour. Sift the flour, cornstarch, baking powder, and salt into a mixing bowl; set aside.

Separate the eggs. Transfer the yolks to a medium bowl and the whites to a larger one. Add ¼ cup of the sugar and the vanilla extract to the yolks and beat with a mixer on high speed for 5 minutes. Beat the egg whites, gradually adding the last ¼ cup of sugar. Beat on low speed, then on high, until stiff.

Gently fold the yolk mixture into the egg whites. Sprinkle about one third of the flour mixture over the eggs and

fold to mix. Add the remaining flour in two more stages, folding the batter until it is uniformly blended. Then spread the batter evenly in the pan.

Bake for 15 minutes or until the cake is golden brown and springy to the touch. Meanwhile, sift confectioners' sugar over a clean tea towel to cover an area roughly the size of the baking

pan. When the cake is done, invert it onto the tea towel. Immediately peel off the paper and roll the cake and towel up together like a rug. Place the roll on a wire rack, seam down, and cool.

Unroll the cake. In a bowl, stir the preserves to a smooth consistency, then spread them evenly over the cake. Snugly reroll the cake — this time without the towel — and transfer it to a serving plate. Sift confectioners' sugar over the cake. Slice with a serrated knife. Serves 8.

Cinnamon Coffee Cake

This sour-cream coffee cake, with pockets of sweet cinnamon, makes a lovely gift for neighbors.

INGREDIENTS

Cinnamon filling:

1	tablespoon cinnamon
4	tablespoons softened butter
$1/3$	cup brown sugar
2	tablespoons all-purpose flour

Coffee cake:

3	cups all-purpose flour
2	teaspoons baking powder
$1/2$	teaspoon baking soda
$1/2$	teaspoon salt
$1/2$	cup butter, at room temperature
$1^1/2$	cups sugar
3	eggs
2	teaspoons vanilla extract
1	16-ounce container sour cream
	Confectioners' sugar

Heat the oven to 350° and grease a 12-cup bundt pan. To make the cinnamon filling, place the cinnamon, butter, brown sugar, and flour in a small bowl and mix with your fingers.

For the cake, combine the flour, baking powder, baking soda, and salt in a large mixing bowl. In a separate large bowl, cream the butter and sugar, then beat in the eggs, one at a time. Beat in the vanilla extract and the sour cream. Gradually add the dry ingredients, beating well after each addition.

Spoon half of the coffee cake batter into the bundt pan. Crumble the cinnamon mixture over the top. Pour in the remaining batter and use a table knife to swirl the cinnamon throughout. Bake for 50 to 60 minutes or until a toothpick

inserted comes out clean. Invert the cake onto a rack and cool. Dust with confectioners' sugar. Serves 8 to 10.

★ PARTY FOOD

Easy Ice-cream Pie

For a holiday treat, make a frozen pie with your favorite green ice cream.

INGREDIENTS

- 1¹/₂ cups finely crushed graham crackers or chocolate wafers
- 5 tablespoons melted butter
- 1 quart softened pistachio or mint chocolate chip ice cream
- ¹/₂ cup hot fudge sauce, store-bought or homemade (see recipe at right)
- 2 cups whipped cream
  Red and green candies

Place the graham crackers or chocolate wafers in a 9-inch pie pan. Stir in the butter, then press the mixture into the bottom and sides of the pan. Freeze for 30 minutes.

Fill with the quart of ice cream, layer on ¹/₂ cup of hot fudge sauce, top with whipped cream, and sprinkle with red and green candies. Freeze before slicing and serving. Makes 1 pie.

★ PARTY FOOD
TREE-SICLES

Make a forest of these tree treats using pints of ice cream. Set a pint, still in the carton, on its side and cut it in half. Cut or peel the container away from the disk of ice cream. Insert a Popsicle stick halfway in one side. With a warm butter knife, trim the disk into a tree shape with the stick as the trunk. Drizzle on thin lines of melted chocolate garlands, then press on M&M's Minis for lights.

★ GIFT FROM THE KITCHEN

Hot Fudge Sundae Pack

The words "gift" and "chocolate" should be synonymous. That is what *FamilyFun* contributing editor Jodi Picoult's mother-in-law Rachel thinks. She modified this hot fudge sauce from *The Silver Palate Cookbook*'s version, and it became a family favorite. It supposedly can keep for several weeks in the fridge, although she admits it has never lasted long enough for her to know that for sure!

INGREDIENTS

- 4 ounces unsweetened chocolate
- 3 tablespoons sweet butter
- ²/₃ cup boiling water
- 1²/₃ cups sugar
- 6 tablespoons corn syrup
- 1 tablespoon vanilla extract
  Mason jar and label stickers
  Ice cream dish and spoon (optional)

Melt the chocolate and butter on low heat in a heavy saucepan. Carefully add boiling water to the melted butter/chocolate mix and stir well. Add the sugar and corn syrup and stir until smooth. Turn up the heat to medium and stir until the mix starts to boil, then maintain the heat just at the boiling point for 9 minutes. Remove the sauce from the heat and let it cool for 15 minutes. Stir in the vanilla extract.

Pour the sauce into two microwave-safe jars. Add a card explaining that the fudge should be stored in the refrigerator and reheated before serving (try the microwave for 30 seconds or so). Makes 2 cups — plus extra for the cooks!

Present your hot fudge in jars that can be reheated in the microwave. We used mason jars (the lids would be removed before reheating, of course). Plastic jars and tubs can also work. We show a pint jar here (it's for some really good friends), but smaller sizes will still seem generous, as a little hot fudge goes a long way. Make a custom label from card stock and double-sided tape or purchase label stickers at an office supply or craft store. To add a bit more indulgence to the gift, include a set of ice-cream dishes and spoons.

Chocolate Mint Brownies

When wrapped and tied with a ribbon, these fudgelike brownies — with their cheerful layer of mint frosting — look like a pretty, edible package.

INGREDIENTS

Brownies:

1/2	cup butter
4	ounces unsweetened chocolate
1 1/2	cups sugar
3	eggs
1 1/2	teaspoons vanilla extract
1	cup all-purpose flour
1/2	teaspoon salt

Mint Frosting:

1/4	cup softened butter
2 1/2	cups confectioners' sugar
1 1/2	to 3 tablespoons milk
1/2	teaspoon peppermint extract
	Green food coloring

Chocolate Topping:

3/4	cup semisweet chocolate chips
3	tablespoons butter

Heat the oven to 350° and grease a 9-inch square baking pan. For the brownies, place the butter and chocolate in a microwave-safe bowl and cook on high for 1 minute, stir, cook for 1 minute more, then stir until smooth. In a separate bowl, whisk together the sugar and eggs. Stir in the chocolate and the vanilla extract. Finally, stir in the flour and salt. Pour into the greased pan and bake for 25 minutes or until a knife inserted in the middle comes out clean. Cool for 1 hour.

For the frosting, cream the butter and confectioners' sugar. Add the milk 1 tablespoon at a time, beating until it is smooth and spreadable. Beat in the peppermint extract and tint to the desired shade with green food coloring. Frost the cooled brownies, cover, and chill for 1 hour.

To make the topping, put the chocolate chips and butter in a microwave-safe bowl and microwave on high for 1½ minutes or until the chocolate melts. Stir until smooth. Pour the chocolate over the brownies and smooth it with a knife. Refrigerate for 45 minutes or until the coating hardens.

Bring the brownies to room temperature, then cut into 16 to 32 pieces. Layer them on a piece of cellophane (with waxed paper between the layers to prevent sticking), wrap up the brownie package, and tie with a ribbon. Makes 16 to 32 brownies.

Chocolate Church Mice

Peanut ears, M&M's eyes, and licorice tails transform these chocolate-covered apricots into sweet little mice — ones that will scurry out of your gift box and into eager mouths.

INGREDIENTS

1	cup semisweet chocolate chips
1	tablespoon vegetable shortening
48	dried apricots
	Wooden skewers
48	M&M's Minis
	Black shoestring licorice
24	dry-roasted peanut halves

Place the chocolate chips and shortening in a microwave-safe bowl and microwave on high for 1 minute. Stir and microwave for 1 minute more. Stir until smooth. For each mouse, press together 2 dried apricots, making a

small point for the mouse's nose, and thread them onto a skewer. Dip them into the melted chocolate and place on a waxed-paper-lined baking sheet. Use a second skewer to push the mouse off the first skewer; use your fingertip to cover the hole left behind with chocolate. Add M&M's Minis eyes, a shoestring licorice tail, and peanut ears (we broke each peanut half in half again). Refrigerate until hardened. Makes 24.

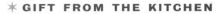

Muddy Snowballs

To make this version of Snowballs, the classic holiday cookie, kids get to throw them in "mud" — a dust of cocoa and confectioners' sugar.

INGREDIENTS

Cookies:

1	cup (2 sticks) unsalted butter, softened
2	ounces unsweetened chocolate, melted and cooled
2/3	cup confectioners' sugar
1	egg yolk
1 1/2	teaspoons vanilla extract
2	cups all-purpose flour
1/4	teaspoon salt
3/4	cup finely chopped walnuts

Dust:

3/4	cup confectioners' sugar
3	tablespoons unsweetened cocoa powder

In a large bowl, using a wooden spoon, cream the butter until smooth. Stir in the melted chocolate and blend well. Add the 2/3 cup of confectioners' sugar, egg yolk, and vanilla extract and stir until combined. Stir in the flour and salt until smooth. Add the walnuts and stir until combined. Cover and refrigerate the dough for at least 1 to 2 hours or until it is firm enough to roll into balls.

Heat the oven to 350°. Form scant tablespoonfuls of the dough into 1-inch balls. Place the balls on two ungreased baking sheets, leaving about 1 inch between them. Bake for 10 to 12 minutes or until the tops of the cookies are set. Cool on the baking sheets for about 3 minutes. Repeat until all the dough has been used.

Meanwhile, stir together the 3/4 cup of confectioners' sugar and the cocoa powder in a shallow bowl. Carefully dip the warm cookies into the dust (that is, throw them in the mud) to coat.

Cool the cookies completely on a wire rack. Roll again in the cocoa–confectioners' sugar dust. These snowballs don't need refrigeration — just store in an airtight container. Makes about 4 dozen Muddy Snowballs.

Cookies in a Jar

Give this gift to someone who loves to bake as much as you do. With its layers of colorful ingredients, it is most beautiful unwrapped.

INGREDIENTS

1/4	cup sugar
1/2	cup packed brown sugar
1 1/2	cups all-purpose flour
3/4	teaspoon baking soda
1/4	teaspoon baking powder
1/2	cup chocolate-covered candy (such as holiday M&M's or Hershey's Holiday Candy Coated Bits)
1/2	cup rolled oats
1/2	cup cocoa crisped-rice cereal (or regular flavor)
1/2	cup white chocolate chips

In a 1-quart widemouthed jar, add the ingredients in the order listed. Pack them down firmly after each addition (use the blunt end of a table knife or a wooden spoon to level and tamp down each layer). Set aside and prepare a gift tag with the following instructions:

"To make your holiday cookies, cream together 1/2 cup of butter or margarine, 1/2 teaspoon of vanilla extract, and 1 egg in a large bowl. Add the contents of the jar and stir until well blended (expect the mix to be dry, but add a few tablespoons of water if necessary to combine). Drop by rounded teaspoonfuls onto an ungreased cookie sheet. Bake at 350° for 10 to 12 minutes. Makes 4 dozen."

Create a tag from a folded rectangle of white card stock, decorate it with markers, and write the baking directions on the inside. Punch a hole in the corner for a length of ribbon, which can then be tied around the jar's neck or secured beneath the threads of the lid.

HOME, SWEET HOME

For more exterior decorating of your chalet, try any of the ideas below — or head to the candy aisle and dream up your own.

Gumdrops Set these out as boulders and shrubs or join with pretzel sticks to make a low fence.

Red Hot Candies Perfect for tree decorations, holly berries, house trim, and snowman noses.

Caramels Use these as stepping-stones or stack them up to make a stovepipe.

Fruit Roll-Up Roll this out as a pathway or cut it to make flags and banners.

Swedish Fish Layer these as roof tiles or stand them on end as a colorful fence.

Starburst Use these to make brick paths, fences, or wishing wells.

Pretzel Sticks Pile up as firewood or use for fencing, roofing, or siding.

Licorice Lace Outline doors and windows or string up as holiday lights.

Marshmallows Pile up a few as a snowbank or stack together three for a snowman.

Necco Wafers These colorful disks make great siding, roof tiles, or flagstones.

Skittles Use these to make house trim, holiday lights, roof tiles, or doorknobs.

Graham Crackers Great for shutters, pathways, skis, docks, and signs.

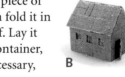

✳ **GIFTS FROM THE KITCHEN**

Graham Cracker Chalet

As any builder will tell you, gingerbread house construction is traditionally tricky. But not so with this Alpine chalet. Made from a revolutionary new building material — graham crackers — it's a cinch for even first-time home builders.

MATERIALS

- Craft knife and scissors
- Cardboard six-pack container
- Masking tape
- Yellow cellophane
- Flashlight
- Corrugated cardboard
- Store-bought frosting
- Graham crackers
- Pretzel nibs, sugar wafers, and assorted candies (for decorating)
- Golden Grahams cereal

Basic structure: Using a craft knife (a parent's job), cut out windows on the long sides of the container. Tape a square of cellophane inside each window. From one of the short sides, cut out a door to one side of the center seam. To make sure the flashlight will fit inside, try putting it through this door (cut out some of the inner structure so you can center the light). Onto the corrugated cardboard, trace and cut out a peaked wall for each short end of the container (see A). From one peaked wall, cut out a hinged door in the same place as the one on the container. Tape both cardboard walls in place. Cut out a 12- by 9-inch piece of cardboard, then fold it in half for the roof. Lay it on top of the container, trimming if necessary, and tape in place.

Siding: Starting at the front of the house and ending with the roof, apply icing to each surface using a butter knife, then press on graham crackers (see B). (**Tip:** Leave a ¼-inch margin along the bottom of the house. The crackers may settle as they dry.) Resize any crackers that don't fit by nibbling!

Trim: Now you can decorate your house however you like, using icing to affix the decorations. We used rows of pretzel nibs and sugar wafer cookies on the walls, accented with mini marshmallows and licorice-twist trim.

Roof: Cover one side of the roof with icing. Apply the bottom-most row of Golden Grahams, then overlap each successive layer, working upward. Repeat for the other side. Add a licorice ridgepole. For the chimney base, cut 2 Starburst candies in half diagonally and attach them to the roof with icing mortar. Top with more Starburst bricks. Use scissors (parents only) to cut long, thin triangles from the large marshmallows. Attach these along the eaves with icing.

Final touches: Add any other decorations you like, such as starlight mint ornaments, a Life Savers wreath, or confectioners' sugar snow. Allow all frosting to dry, then turn on the flashlight and slide it inside the house.

Cereal Ball Ornament

For a sweet twist on the classic popcorn ball, mix multicolored cereal with melted marshmallows and shape into Christmas balls. Wrapped in plastic and tied with a ribbon, they will look great on your tree — if they make it out of the kitchen!

INGREDIENTS

3	tablespoons butter
1	10-ounce bag marshmallows
8	cups colorful cereal, such as Trix
	Plastic wrap
	Ribbon

Before beginning, butter a large mixing bowl and a sheet of waxed paper. Then, in a saucepan over medium heat, melt the 3 tablespoons of butter and stir in the marshmallows (have kids ages ten and up wear an oven mitt and stir with a long-handled spoon). Stir the mixture until the marshmallows have melted.

Pour the marshmallow mixture into the prepared bowl (the mixture will be extremely hot; this is a job for parents only). Add the cereal and, using a rubber spatula, stir until evenly combined. Cool the mixture for 3 to 5 minutes.

Have your child butter her hands. She should then take about ¾ cup of the cereal mixture and shape it into a colorful ball, patting the surface smooth. Place each ball on the buttered waxed paper. (If the mixture sticks to your child's hands, she may have to butter her hands again.)

Cool the balls, allowing them to set, before wrapping them individually in plastic wrap. Make a bow at the top of each ball with a piece of ribbon, then tie on another piece for hanging on the tree. Makes 14 balls.

Celebration Sticks

Celebrate the colors of Kwanzaa with these sprinkle-coated pretzel sticks. Your kids can hand them out to friends during Kwanzaa.

INGREDIENTS

	Red, green, and black (or chocolate) sprinkles
1	cup white chocolate chips
20	8-inch pretzel rods
	Ribbon

On waxed paper, arrange 1¼-inch-wide stripes of the sprinkles, as shown. In a shallow microwave-safe bowl, microwave the white chocolate chips on high for 1 minute, stir, and microwave for 30 seconds

more. Stir until smooth. Use a knife to spread the chocolate over half of a pretzel rod. Roll through the sprinkles until coated with stripes. Chill. To present the sticks, bundle them with ribbon. Makes 20.

SNOWMEN STICKS

Dressed in colorful candy scarves and top hats, these stylish, easy-to-make snowmen are sure to liven up any holiday gathering. To make a batch, melt 1 cup of white chocolate chips in the top of a double boiler.

One at a time, dip one end of an 8-inch pretzel rod in the melted chocolate and use a plastic spoon or knife to spread it two thirds of the way down the rod. Set the pretzels on a sheet of waxed paper and press on mini chocolate chips for eyes and buttons. Use orange decorators' gel to add a carrot nose.

When the chocolate has hardened, stand the pretzels in a mug or glass and tie on strips of fruit leather for scarves. For each hat, stretch a gummy ring over the narrow end of a gumdrop and secure it on the pretzel rod with a dab of melted chocolate.

✳ QUICK TREAT

Chocolate Mice

Here's how to make some nice mice for your tree. For each mouse, remove the tags from two Hershey's Kisses.

MATERIALS

Pink felt
Double-sided carpet tape
Hershey's Kisses
Fishing line (for hanging)
Self-adhesive googly eyes
4-inch piece of curling ribbon

Cut out mouse ears from pink felt, about ⅜ inch high. Using the double-sided tape, affix the bottoms of the ears to the flat side of one of the Kisses. Tape an 8-inch loop of fishing line behind the ears for hanging on your tree. With more double-sided tape, join together the two flat sides of 2 Hershey's Kisses, with the mouse ears and fishing line loop pointing up. Add a pair of self-adhesive googly eyes. Slip a tail — the curling ribbon — under the foil. Now, see how they run (or disappear) from your tree!

✳ GIFT FROM THE KITCHEN

Chocolate Granola Clusters

This old-time recipe makes a great primer for young holiday-cookie makers, since there's no baking involved. Instead, the chocolate coating is simmered on the stovetop and then stirred into the granola to create melt-in-your-mouth morsels.

INGREDIENTS

2	cups granola
¼	cup milk
4	tablespoons butter
⅓	cup sugar
¼	cup chocolate chips
¼	cup peanut butter
½	teaspoon vanilla extract
	Yogurt-covered raisins or peanuts

Have your child measure the granola into a large mixing bowl and then break up any clusters into small pieces with his fingers. Line a large baking sheet with waxed paper.

Warm the milk and butter in a medium saucepan over moderate heat. When the butter is mostly melted, use a long-handled wooden spoon to stir in the sugar and chocolate chips. Continue to stir the mixture carefully until it comes to a boil, then quickly reduce the heat and cook the sauce at a low boil for 1 minute. Remove the pan from the heat and stir in the peanut butter and vanilla extract until smooth.

Immediately pour the sauce over the

granola and stir well. Scoop mounded tablespoons of the mixture onto the lined baking sheet, leaving a little space between each one. Gently press a yogurt-covered raisin or peanut into each mound. Once the cookies have cooled completely, cover them with plastic wrap and refrigerate them for at least 3 hours before serving. Makes about 2 dozen cookies.

Paper Bag Luminarias, page 60

CHAPTER THREE

Holiday Celebrations

'TIS THE SEASON to be jolly — and to invite friends to join in your holiday festivities. Whether you're planning a classroom party, an informal family get-together, or a merry houseful of caroling kids, we know that great parties call for great ideas — ideas, especially, that kids can get in on.

So, on the following pages, we present our ultimate guide to holiday parties — party games and activities, simple menus, and complete plans. Such as? A silly reindeer game that all the kids will want to play (page 59), creative Gift-swapping Games (page 58), and a glittering party hat for Three Kings Day (page 67). We hope each idea will help your family and guests celebrate the season in all its fullness, sparkle, and joy.

Start with a basic party plan. Throwing a party doesn't have to be expensive or exhausting — and the memories you create can last a lifetime. To make sure that everyone has a good time (including you), keep the guest list to a manageable size, use the holiday decorations you already have in place, and come up with a creative theme, such as a holiday cookie party instead of a complete sit-down dinner.

Send invitations early. In the midst of a season of parties, it's a good idea to let friends know the date of your party at least three weeks in advance. In addition to the date and time of the party, specify the theme in your invitation as well as any items guests should bring.

Enlist help. Ask your spouse, relatives, or even your children's baby-sitter for support both in planning and hosting the party. And don't forget to involve your children in the party preparation — to them, getting ready for the party can be as exciting as the big event.

Time it well. If you are hosting younger kids , start the event between 3 and 5 in the afternoon, after kids have had their naps and there are still hours before bedtime. In the same vein, you may want to wrap it up after about four hours when kids, and parents, start needing some downtime.

Make the party hands-on. To allow the adults time to socialize, keep little hands occupied with a simple holiday activity, such as making the Reindeer Hats (page 59), playing the dreidel game (page 61), or decorating baked sugar cookies (page 45). Party crafts and treats also make excellent take-home favors.

Go with the flow. Once the party begins, follow your basic party plan but remain flexible. If something doesn't go as planned, roll with the punches and change activities, and your party will be a winner.

TREE-TRIMMING PARTY

With all the excitement in the air, a party can be a hit just by offering good food and good fellowship. But if you are entertaining kids, parents will appreciate a gathering that offers a little more. That's the idea behind this ornament-making party. Making ornaments is an activity that's easy enough for every age to have fun with — and talk about instant party favors! Preparation is relatively simple. Just pick a few of the following ideas you like:

Crafts: Make Holiday Garlands (below), Baby Sock Snowman (page 15), or My Little Angel (page 28).

Games: Play Pin the Nose on Rudolph (page 59) or Gift-swapping Games (page 58).

Menu: Serve Hot Cider (page 34), Wrap 'n' Stack Tree (page 40), and decorate-your-own Dancing Ginger People (page 36).

✴ PARTY ACTIVITY

Holiday Garlands

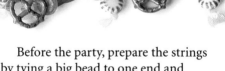

Garlands turned out to be the hit of *FamilyFun* contributor Jenifer Harm's tree-trimming party. Basically, says Jenifer, if you can poke a needle through it, you can string it on a garland. Before your party, set out an assortment of inedible and edible materials. If you want, you can invite your friends to string garlands potluck style and ask everyone to contribute a few stringables.

MATERIALS
   Heavy-duty thread or ribbon
   Large beads
   Tapestry needle
Candy Garland:
   Wrapped peppermint candy, pretzel
      twists, gumdrops, Life Savers

candies (assorted colors), and red licorice (cut up the long pieces)
Natural Garland:
   Dried orange slices (available at craft supply stores), popcorn, pinecones (wrap twine between scales to hold in place), cinnamon sticks, and cranberries
Bead Garland:
   Wooden beads, felt stars, and colorful buttons

Before the party, prepare the strings by tying a big bead to one end and threading a large, dull needle (tapestry needles work well) onto the other. For manageability, don't make the strings longer than the kids are tall.

Set out the materials in separate bowls. Invite guests to string their own garlands.

Mr. Sandman

Scented with holiday spices, our scroll-bearing sandpaper gingerbread folks couldn't be a more inviting way to get out the word about your holiday party. And when they're finished with their party come-hithers, these charming messengers become great tree ornaments.

MATERIALS

- Sandpaper (finer grits are easier to cut)
- Glue
- Brown construction paper
- Cinnamon stick and whole nutmeg
- Gingerbread person cookie cutter
- Cardboard
- Puffy paint
- Hole punch
- Ribbon, ⅛ inch wide
- 2½- by 8-inch strip of paper (one per invitation)
- Envelope

To cover the back of the sandpaper, coat it with glue, press on the construction paper, and flatten it under a book to dry. Rub the sandpaper hard all over with the cinnamon stick and then with the nutmeg; this will scent it deliciously. Now make a template by tracing around the cookie cutter onto cardboard and cutting out the shape. Trace around the template on the back of the sandpaper and cut out as many people as you need (we got about four gingerbread people per 9- by 11-inch sheet of sandpaper).

Use puffy paint to add details and decorations and let the paint dry. With a hole punch, make a hole in the top of the head and in one of the hands, then thread a length of ribbon through the head and knot. Now write your invitation on the strip of paper, roll it scroll-like, and fit it through the cookie person's hand. Flatten the scroll slightly and pop the cookie person in an envelope.

SHELF ELVES

Line up a few of these elves on a windowsill or mantel, and you're guaranteed to spread cheer to family and guests alike.

For each elf, fill a colored cotton sock three quarters of the way with dried peas or beans. An easy way to do this is to cut the bottom from a paper cup, then insert the bottomless cup into the neck of the sock. Pour the beans through the makeshift funnel.

With a needle and thread, stitch closed the top of the sock. Use a few more stitches to gather and secure the sewn end into a point that resembles the tip of a stocking hat. Then sew a medium-size jingle bell to the tip.

Now it's time to form the elf's nose (a fun job for kids). Using your fingertips, grasp a small bunch of beans about halfway down from the top of the sock. Wrap a rubber band around the base of the bunch to secure it. Finally, glue or sew on two button eyes.

Preholiday Party

"Last year in mid-November, some friends and I got our five-year-olds together for a crafty pre-Christmas party. They made gift wrap by sponge-painting star and tree shapes in red and green paint on plain brown paper. Then they decorated white and brown paper sacks to make Santa, bear, and snowman gift bags. To put us in the holiday spirit, we listened to Christmas music and snacked on cookies. The party was such fun and the gift wrap and bags were so special that we're doing it again this year."

— Kim Johnson
Cullman, Alabama

★ PARTY FAVOR

Holiday Crackers

These cheerful candy-filled cardboard tubes, modeled after traditional British crackers, are a snap to mass-produce for a classroom holiday party. Your child can personalize them by inserting mini handwritten notes or drawings along with the candy or adding some noise by tying a jingle bell on one end.

MATERIALS

Wrapping paper

Empty cardboard tubes, trimmed to
    desired lengths

Clear tape or glue stick

Ribbon or string

Wrapped candy, toys, or treats

Jingle bells (optional)

Cut a piece of wrapping paper that's 6 inches longer than the tube and wide enough to wrap completely around it at least once. Center the tube along one long side of the paper and use tape or glue to hold it in place. Your child can then wrap the paper tightly around the tube and secure the seam with tape or glue. She should then twist the excess paper at one end and tie it closed with ribbon or string. Fill the tube with candy and other tiny surprises, then twist and tie closed the open end.

★ PARTY GAME

Gift-swapping Games

Unless your last name is Claus, chances are you won't be able to leave something under your tree for every guest. Instead, ask each guest to bring a wrapped gift that costs less than $5. Then try one of these twists on the traditional grab bag.

Secret Santa: Print each guest name on a slip of paper and tuck one name into each invitation. The secret Santa should anonymously bring an unsigned gift to the party where the intended recipient will open it — and try to guess who gave him the present.

Musical Gifts: No one gets left out in this musical chairs spin-off. Have guests stand in a circle with the gift they brought in their hands. Then play a Christmas carol while passing around the packages. When the music stops, each person keeps the gift in his hand.

Yankee Swap: This luck-of-the-draw option is best for older kids. Print a number for each person participating and take turns drawing one. The person who picks Number 1 chooses and unwraps any gift. Number 2 picks and unwraps a gift that he can keep or swap for Number 1's gift. Number 3 then picks a gift to keep or swap with Number 1 or 2, and so on. This continues until the final person has unwrapped and swapped a gift. Then, at long last, Number 1 may take his or her pick of the whole slew of opened gifts.

Reindeer Hats

Craft the latest North Pole couture at your party: reindeer antlers. Finish the look with red face-paint noses.

MATERIALS
- Brown poster board
- Paper clips
- Glitter glue

For each head- band, cut a 1½- by 24-inch long strip of poster board and, for the antlers, two 6- by 9-inch rectangles. Fit the strip to the child's head, remove it, and paper-clip the ends. Sketch antlers on the rectangular pieces and cut them out. Decorate with glitter glue. When dry, staple the antlers to the headband.

✳ **PARTY GAME**

Pin the Nose on Rudolph

Forget about joining in any reindeer games! With our pin-the-tail-on-the-donkey-style contest, Rudolph gets to star in his very own — the perfect party game for one foggy Christmas Eve. Those red dot stickers from the office supply store make superb reindeer noses, although Rudolph is likely to get a terrible case of the measles on his way to schnozzdom.

MATERIALS
- Construction paper
- Glue stick
- Poster board
- Blindfold
- Red dot stickers

Sketch an outline of a reindeer on construction paper, cut it out, and glue it to the poster board (or your kids can use a marker to draw Rudolph directly on the poster board). Remember to leave Rudolph noseless! To play, hang the picture on a wall, blindfold the kids one at a time, hand each a red sticker, and let them try to return Rudy's shiny nose.

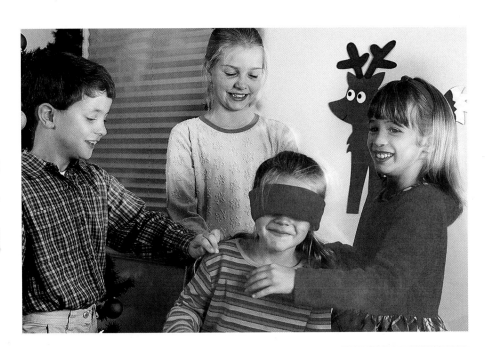

◆ **FAMILYFUN READER TRADITION**

A Winter's Tale

"I always keep a roll of white paper on hand so that when my kids get bored I can tape a large piece to the wall and let them draw a mural. This past Christmas, however, our mural-making took on a new twist. My daughter Emily, age seven, was particularly restless one day when I pulled out the trusty mural paper. She went to work using a new package of markers, and an hour later she had created a masterpiece, complete with manger, carolers, and Santa. It was so festive that we framed it with Christmas ribbon and — for the next few weeks — asked visitors to add to the scene. Emily and her sister Lauren, age five, were tickled to see friends of all ages try a hand at drawing. Even Grandpa — who insists there's not an artistic bone in his body — had fun putting himself inside a house, waving from a window. It became a delightful record of all our visitors during the holiday season."

— Mindy Starns Clark
Mount Royal, New Jersey

Light a Remembrance Candle

Gone for most of us are the days when the entire family assembled for the holidays at Grandma's. Today, Grandma is just as likely to live across two time zones, as are uncles, aunts, and cousins. So how do you bring loved ones together? The Console family of Malden, Missouri, inspired us with a tradition they devised: each year on December 12th (a birthday shared by a grandmother and two cousins), family members get together in spirit by lighting a candle and wishing one another a long-distance happy holiday.

To make the tradition your own, set a date for the big event and send invitations to all involved. Ask that everyone light a candle and send out wishes at an appointed hour (take time zones into account). To add resonance to the candle lighting, play some favorite holiday music and pass around mugs of hot cider.

Paper Bag Luminarias

When moonlighting as luminarias, these lunch bags do a great job leading guests down the path to your holiday party with style.

MATERIALS
Brown paper lunch bag
Hole punch
Sand
Votive candle

To make one, decorate a brown paper lunch bag by tracing a simple pattern in pencil on one side, then punching out your design with a hole punch. Fill each luminaria with about 2 inches of sand and sink a votive candle or tea light in the center. Place the luminarias along a walk, patio, or deck, light them (a grown-up's job), and bask in the glow.

CELEBRATE THE SOLSTICE

It's no wonder that lights are part of every winter celebration. Twinkling against the backdrop of winter's darker days, they stand out as festive and cheery, especially on the longest night of the year: the winter solstice (December 22nd). Marking this day with a simple celebration of light is not only a nice way to teach your kids about the seasons, but it can also be a calming break from the hectic holiday pace.

Keep your celebration down to earth: a candlelit dinner or trip into the backyard to stargaze is ideal. But to really banish the darkness, set aside an hour or so to make our Paper Bag Luminarias, below.

Christmas Party in a Box

"When my seven-year-old son, Jacob, included a Christmas Party in a Box on last year's wish list, I had no idea how he came up with that idea or what he had in mind. But as the holiday approached and I remembered the letdown that kids often feel after opening their presents, I realized that he'd actually come up with a great gift for the whole family. I bought a snowman piñata, filled it with small toys and candy, and put it in a box with holiday plates, napkins, window clings, and streamers. I topped off the wrapped box with a balloon bouquet and a note that read 'Do not open until Grandpa and Grandma arrive.' The kids were thrilled when they opened it, and they decorated the house while I finished preparing our meal. Later, we all had fun with the piñata. Before he went to bed that night, Jacob said that he knew what he wanted next year — another Christmas Party in a Box."

— Amy Waltz
Richmond, Indiana

Hanukkah Party

A few days before Hanukkah begins, the Skolnick family unpacks all their decorations (the clay dreidel, the glow-in-the-dark dreidel, the silver and blue garlands, Stars of David, and assorted Hanukkah flags). In no time, their Upper East Side Manhattan apartment is decked out with the symbols of the season. After the decorations are up, the family celebrates the holiday in earnest. Each night, candles are lit and blessings said. The Skolnicks usually hold at least one Hanukkah party themselves and attend several others. They might play games with one of their many dreidels (for rules, see below). At the parties, they devour the food they've looked forward to eating all year long — including latkes and the Israeli *sufganiyot* (a kind of jelly doughnut cooked in oil). But for mom Susan, their decorations are the necessary warm-up. "It's a big part of what makes the holiday ours," she says.

✳ HANUKKAH GAME

Play Dreidel

One of the most popular Hanukkah pastimes is playing the dreidel game. It is a form of an old German gambling game, and its name derives from the German word for "top." The stakes are decidedly low-key during Hanukkah, however, with players betting their fortune in chocolates or pennies with each spin of the dreidel. The top has four sides, each marked with a Hebrew character: *nun, gimel, heh,* and *shin.* The letters also stand for the Hebrew phrase *Nes Gadol Haya Sham,* or "A great miracle happened here."

MATERIALS
Dreidel
Objects for the pot, such as chocolate coins, Hershey's Kisses, buttons, raisins, nuts, or pennies

Evenly divide the betting objects among all players. Before each spin of the dreidel, each player antes up by placing one item into the pot. The first player spins the dreidel. There are four possible outcomes. For instance, if *nun* comes up, the player gets nothing and the next player takes a spin. If *gimel,*

Gimel: If your spin turns up this side of the dreidel, you are a winner — take the whole pot!

Nun: If the dreidel lands on nun, you don't get anything at all and it is the next player's turn.

heh, or *shin* comes up, see the chart below. All players ante up again before the next person spins. Whenever the pot is empty or has only one object left in it, each player has to ante up again before the next spin. The game is over when one player has everything and everyone else is cleaned out.

Heh: If you spin and the dreidel falls on heh, you can scoop up half the items from the pot.

Shin: With this unluckiest roll, you must put an item in the pot and let the next player spin.

✦ FAMILYFUN WRITER TRADITION

Kwanzaa Party

"We've celebrated Kwanzaa for nearly a decade, but one year that stands out in my mind was the year my brother-in-law, Leon, came up with an impromptu activity that brought even greater relevance to the spirit of unity and family togetherness that is the true meaning of the holiday. Leon gathered everyone in a circle and lit a large candle in the center. He asked each of us to call forth the name of a loved one or notable African American who had passed on, yet whose memory still remains, or whose contributions still touch our culture. Some of us named elders who had passed away during the year. Others called out the names of people such as Harriet Tubman and Martin Luther King, Jr., women and men whom we consider part of our larger African American family. The glow of the single candle at the circle's center was to honor the flame that these people keep alive in each of us."

— Andrea Davis Pinkney
Brooklyn, New York

✳ PARTY DECORATION

Kwanzaa Kinara

Inspired by a centuries-old African harvest festival, Kwanzaa is a celebration of African American heritage, culture, and community. Traditions include fasting, feasting, reflection, gift exchanging, and discussion of the seven principles, from unity to creativity. On each of the seven days, a new candle is lit on the kinara. If your family plans to celebrate Kwanzaa, craft this elegant candleholder — and keep it for many years to come.

MATERIALS
   One 14-inch length of 1- by 2-inch wood
   Silver acrylic paint and paintbrush
   Tacky glue and cotton swab
   One 1½-inch-long ⅝-inch cap screw
   Seven ⅝-inch hex nuts
   Glitter, sequins, gemstones, and other decorations (optional)
   Seven 8-inch taper candles (1 black, 3 red, and 3 green), trimmed to fit
   Candle shaver (optional)

   Trim and sand the wood, if necessary, then paint it silver and let it dry. Next, glue one screw-and-nut combo to the middle of the base and space three nuts evenly on each side. Use a cotton swab to spread a little glue on the threads of the middle nut and attach it to the screw with a single turn, leaving enough room for a candle to fit inside.

   Decorate the base with sequins and gemstones, if you like, and let the kinara dry.

   Add the candles, arranged so that the black one is in the middle, with red and green on either side. Shave the candles, if necessary, to fit.

   Before you light your candles each night, explain to your kids the principle the candle represents: unity (black candle), self-determination (red), collective work and responsibility (green), cooperative economics (red), purpose (green), creativity (red), and faith (green).

Merry Mice Race

It won't take long for this raring mice game to win over *Nutcracker* party guests. Let the kids take the mice game pieces home as party favors.

MATERIALS
- Felt and thread
- Walnut shells
- Hot glue gun
- Markers
- Marbles

To make each mouse, fold in half small felt circles for ears. Glue together the lower portion of each ear, leaving the back open. Glue the ears, a felt tail, and whiskers of thread onto a shell half. Lastly, use a colored marker to draw on eyes and a nose.

To play, place a marble under the walnut shell bodies, set them on a smooth, inclined surface, and watch the mice race each other to the finish.

The Story of the Nutcracker

According to German folklore, the grim, if not fierce, appearance of traditional nutcrackers was no matter of chance. They were said to protect a family's home by baring their teeth to evil spirits. The practice of collecting them became popular in the United States in the 1950s when American GIs brought them home. Originally fashioned after kings and military officers, nutcrackers today (which involve up to 130 steps to make) look like soccer players, Egyptian pharaohs, American presidents, or even Santa Claus.

✷ **PARTY PLAN**

NUTCRACKER PARTY

It's that time of year when sugarplum fairies and mice kings charm audiences nationwide in performances of the holiday ballet *The Nutcracker*. Even if your family can't get tickets to a live show, you can still make a night of it by hosting this *Nutcracker* party:

Entertainment: **Pick up a videotaped version, such as the one by Mikhail Baryshnikov and the American Ballet Theater (MGM/UA Home Video), at a local video store or library. Or, plan the event for the same date as a televised production.**

Craft: **Make Snappy Soldiers (page 31).**

Menu: **Serve Chocolate Mice (page 53) and sugarplum punch (grape juice and seltzer).**

Activity: **Don't forget to make room for impromptu dance-along performances.**

Holiday Storytelling

At this year's holiday bash, entertain guests with a lively storytelling session. Or, start a new family Advent tradition — and read a holiday book every night until Christmas.

MATERIALS

Slips of paper

Markers

Holiday children's stories

Gather several holiday books or ask guests to bring them to the party (for ideas, see the list below). Write the title of each book on a scrap of paper and put them all in a bowl. When everyone is settled in for the storytelling session, take turns picking a title out of the jar and reading that book. (Prereading guests can choose a reader for the book they pick.) For longer works, like *A Christmas Carol*, select an individual chapter or a short passage. Set a limit on each guest's reading time, maybe five minutes.

To keep the storytelling lively, give kids a refrain to say, such as "ho, ho, ho," and agree on a signal, such as a raised finger, that cues them. Or, suggest that everyone say the refrain whenever someone mentions the word "snow" or "Santa."

Holiday Stories

✦ *The Night Before Christmas* by Clement C. Moore
✦ *A Christmas Carol* by Charles Dickens
✦ *The Polar Express* by Chris Van Allsburg
✦ *Seven Candles for Kwanzaa* by Andrea Davis Pinkney
✦ *Inside-Out Grandma* by Joan Rothenberg
✦ *Coyote Christmas* by Tom Robertson
✦ The New Testament
✦ *How the Grinch Stole Christmas* by Dr. Seuss
✦ *The Twelve Cats of Christmas* by Kandy Radzinski
✦ *Rudolph the Red-nosed Reindeer*

A BIRTHDAY PARTY

For some of the readers of *FamilyFun*, throwing a birthday party for Jesus is a fun way to remind children of the meaning of Christmas. We especially like the party devised by the Pryor family — Tammy and Tim and their kids Travis, Ryan, and Jessica — of Las Vegas, Nevada. Like most birthday celebrations, theirs features decorations, cake, games, a chorus of "Happy Birthday," and presents. But instead of Barbie dolls and action figures, the gifts at this party might be coats and blankets for the homeless, ornaments for a senior citizens' center, or stuffed animals for a children's hospital (eight-year-old Travis's idea).

At the gathering, guests wrap and sometimes craft presents and, after the festivities, help deliver the gifts. When the Pryors threw their first party five years ago, it was mostly a family affair; now, it's grown to include the children of family and friends — 35 to 40 guests strong. And while the party itself is a blast, Tammy reports, the real treat isn't playing games or eating birthday cake, but the simple joy of giving.

Caroling Party

Organizing a caroling party in your neighborhood — or at a nursing home or senior center — is a wonderful way to give the gift of friendship during the holiday season, and to get into the Christmas spirit.

Begin by arranging a time and place for the event (check the Yellow Pages for senior centers and nursing homes in your area, then contact the activities coordinator at one of the places to set a date).

When assembling a party of carolers, include neighbors, friends of your family, or classmates of your children. Invite carolers to bring photocopies of their favorite holiday songs (or download them from the Internet). At the rehearsal, decide on the order of songs and arrange any instrumental accompaniment that members of the group may have to offer. Keep in mind that most senior centers and nursing homes have a recreation room with a piano; finding someone willing to accompany the carolers will be well worth the effort. You also may want to invest in a few simple instruments, such as triangles, shakers, or bells.

Several days before the performance, drop off kid-made invitations to be distributed to the residents or guests. On the day of the caroling party, arrive early, set up a few festive decorations, and put out cookies and juice for the carolers and listeners. You can pass out extra lyrics so the audience can sing along.

After the concert, encourage your kids to be social and friendly with the residents and guests. Don't forget to clean up before you leave.

Countdown Goodie Bags

For fun that lasts all night long on New Year's Eve, assemble bags with party favors, prizes, and other surprises. Guests at your New Year's bash will love opening a new bag every hour.

MATERIALS

Colorful paper bags
Construction paper
Markers, stickers, and glue
Inexpensive prizes

Before the party, assemble a bag for every hour until midnight. You might fill one bag with inexpensive plastic watches so guests will know the minute it's midnight. Fill another bag with notepads, plus colorful markers so guests can write down their New Year's resolutions. In a third bag, put a disposable instant camera and a note that asks the kids to snap pictures of each other. The last bag should be filled with noisemakers and party crackers (and opened a few minutes before midnight!) So that the partyers know when to open each bag, write different times 7 P.M., 8 P.M., 9 P.M., and so on) on the front of each bag — or glue on a construction paper clock face, as we did. The kids may want to set an alarm clock to ring hourly to remind them to open the next bag.

* PARTY DECORATION

O New Year's Tree

When Christmas gives way to New Year's, try this creative decorating idea, which comes from *FamilyFun* reader Rhonda Johnstone. Each year, Rhonda and her children, Ethan, Eryn, and Tessa (12, ten, and eight years old, respectively), take down the ornaments from their Christmas tree and give it a makeover.

MATERIALS

Undecorated Christmas tree
Blue ribbon
Party horns and hats
Balloons

✦ FAMILYFUN READER TRADITION

Resolution Stowaways

The Edgerley family of Granville, Illinois — mom Mary, dad Philip, Emily, 12, Rachel, ten, and Philip, nine — has a simple trick for keeping track of their New Year's resolutions. Together, they pen their plans on holiday stationery on New Year's Eve, then tuck them into their Christmas stockings before they're packed away. When the stockings come out of storage the next year, the kids pluck out the lists and put them aside until New Year's Eve when they are shared out loud and replaced with new ones. "I like doing it because it gives you something to look forward to," says Emily, whose resolutions have included things like "I'll try to eat more fruits and vegetables."

Have your kids help you curl the ribbon and make bows. Tie them to the branches, along with party horns and hats and balloons. You can even replace the tree skirt. The only thing you should keep is your string of lights.

Tip: Rhonda points out the convenience of trimming your tree with what's essentially the makings of a New Year's party: "By the time the party's over, the tree will be undecorated!"

Crowns for Kings

The twelfth night of Christmas, which is also called Three Kings Day and Epiphany, calls for special celebration at *FamilyFun* contributing editor Lynne Bertrand's church. She serves cake to the kids in the church school, festively decorated with foil crowns, with a raisin hidden in the center. Whichever child gets the piece of cake with the raisin in it gets to be king for the day. Then all the kids craft these glittery crowns to wear.

MATERIALS

Gold poster board
2 large paper clips
Glitter glue
Pom-poms
Sequins and faux gems
Construction paper and glue

To make the headband-style hat, cut out a strip of poster board about 24 inches long and 3 to 6 inches wide. Cut crown points along one edge of the strip, fit it around your child's forehead, and paper-clip the ends.

Then have the kids decorate the crowns with glitter glue, faux jewels, or cut-out construction paper shapes.

✳ QUICK ACTIVITY

THREE KINGS EVE

Before going to sleep on the eve of January 6th, many children put hay (and a bowl of water) for the Kings' camels in shoe boxes and tuck them under their beds. The next morning, the children wake to find gifts left for them by the Three Kings, such as little chocolates wrapped in gold foil.

✦ FAMILYFUN READER PARTY PLAN

Three Kings Day Party

Not long ago, Kimberly Rivera of New Jersey, started celebrating the holidays the way her grandparents once had in Puerto Rico. "She was born here; she's been Americanized," says her grandfather, Israel Soto. "But we don't want her to lose touch with her culture." Observed on January 6th, Three Kings Day is celebrated mostly in Spain, Latin America, and in the Spanish-speaking part of the Caribbean. The Rivera family started their celebration by leaving a shoe box full of hay under their beds for the Three Kings' camels (see left). The next day they feasted on roast pork and coconut rice and danced along to traditional Puerto Rican songs. The highlight of their party was performing a reenactment of the Three Kings' journey. In the play, a designated king-for-the-day gets to distribute little bags of frankincense, myrrh (woody plants from health food stores), and gold (brass stars) to guests.

CHAPTER FOUR

Gifts Kids Can Make

ASK ANY GRANDPARENT, teacher, or close family friend and she'll tell you that the gifts that mean the most are the ones that come from the heart, and hands, of a child. These one-of-a-kind presents, made with little more than felt and glue and a photograph, are like treasures of childhood and will be cherished for years.

For kids, giving a present that no one else can give is enough to make them swell with pride. And it's the perfect holiday solution: although their buying power may be limited, their imaginations are not. With a simple idea and a few supplies, any child will experience the thrill that comes from giving.

Whether your kids are toddlers or teens, we're sure they'll be inspired by the easy and endearing gifts on the following pages. Here are a few tips to get you started.

Make your holiday list early. Before the season gets into full swing, help your child make a holiday gift-giving list. Then, flip through this chapter and match a gift to each person. The Picture Brooches (page 80) may be ideal for Grandma while the Hand-painted Mug (page 70) would be a welcome gift for a teacher. Once the list is complete, stock up on supplies so that any spare moment can be spent crafting gifts.

**Present Scents,
page 93**

Simplify your gift giving. If you are really pressed for time, choose one gift, such as the Fleece Hat (page 79) or the Mosaic Flowerpot (page 73), and mass-produce it for everyone on your holiday list. With all the supplies laid out, making ten of the same gift doesn't take much longer than making one. It's also smart to craft a few extras and tuck them away for that unexpected visitor who arrives at your door with a wrapped package in hand.

Jazz up your store-bought gifts with homemade gift wrap. Although it would be nice for your child to make and personalize gifts for everyone on her list, obviously it just isn't practical. Instead, have her personalize store-bought gifts with the homemade wrapping paper and gift tags on pages 89, 92, and 93. Or, have her help you make the family greeting card, such as the Punchy Postcards (page 75) or the handprint Family Tree (page 91).

Teach kids the joy of giving. Making gifts introduces kids to the fun and good feeling that come from giving. While your child is working with her hands, encourage her to think about the recipient and add personal touches. In the process, your child will discover the true meaning of the holiday season.

Hand-painted Mugs

Get a handle on your search for that perfect teacher gift by turning a plain mug into a personalized masterpiece. All it takes is some ceramic glaze and a coffee mug. To keep the project cost-efficient, pick up primary colors (red, yellow, and blue) only and mix them into a variety of hues.

MATERIALS

Pebeo Porcelaine 150 glaze (sold at many art supply stores for about $5 for a 1.5-fluid-ounce jar)

Ceramic mug

Scrap paper (for practice)

Watercolor brush or cotton swab

Before your child begins decorating a mug, encourage him to try out a few designs on paper, such as a flower, a snowflake, or polka dots. Once he's settled on one, he can lay the mug on its side and apply the glaze, which is a little thicker than India ink, with a watercolor brush or a cotton swab.

Let the painted mug air-dry for at least 24 hours. Then permanently set the glaze by baking the mug in a preheated 325° oven for 35 minutes.

For a special touch, your child can fill his gift with assorted tea bags or a package of hot chocolate mix.

A Holly, Jolly Apron

Baking Christmas cookies will be even more of a treat when the chef is outfitted in a handsome holiday apron. With this simple potato-printing technique, your child can decorate one for the culinary expert in your family.

MATERIALS

Large potato

Carrot

Craft knife

Paper towels

2 flat bowls

Fabric paint (red and green)

Scrap paper (for practice)

Plain white apron

To begin, cut the potato in half (an adult's job). Then your child can use a pencil to lightly draw a holly leaf on the flat surface, as shown. Help him cut away the parts of the potato around the design and blot it on a paper towel. To prepare the carrot, cut off the tapered end.

Next, pour a thin layer of green paint into a bowl. Have your child press the potato into the paint and practice printing the designs on scrap paper.

When he is ready, he can stamp a pattern of leaves to form a wreath on the front of the apron. For holly berries, he can dip the cut end of the carrot into the red paint (in a separate bowl) and dot the wreath with red prints. Once the paint is dry, follow the fabric paint directions to heat-set the design.

Tip: You and your kids can also accent cloth napkins or a tablecloth with holly prints or a wreath pattern. Or, you may want to create holiday T-shirts or sweatshirts for the whole family.

Dream Weavers

Woven on a small cardboard loom, these colorful coasters make great gifts for a grandparent or teacher.

MATERIALS

8-inch cardboard square
Yarn
Tape
8- by 1½-inch cardboard strip
Plastic tapestry needle

Starting an inch from the upper left corner of the cardboard square, make twelve ½-inch snips spaced a half inch apart (you should end up with a 1-inch margin from the last notch to the right corner). Cut matching notches in the bottom of the loom.

Now help your child thread the loom. Fit and knot an end of a length of yarn into the first upper notch so that a 3-inch tail extends from the back. Bring the yarn down the face of the loom and into the matching notch at the bottom, then up the back side and through the second upper notch. Continue wrapping the yarn around the loom (not too tightly) until all the notches are threaded and you have 12 vertical warp strings. Tape the loose yarn ends to the back of the loom.

Next, slide the 8- by 1½-inch cardboard strip under the tops of the warp strings (this spacer will reserve enough yarn to tie off the finished weave). Then thread yarn through the tapestry needle (sold at most craft stores) and, starting from the middle, weave it over and under alternate warp strings. When you get to one side, start a second full row from that point, this time going under the warp strings you went over the last time and vice versa. Slide the second row snugly up against the first one.

Continue adding full rows until you have woven a coaster-size square. Then weave the end of the strand back into the preceding row. To change colors, simply work the end of the strand you're using back into the weave, then start the next row in the center as you did at the beginning.

To finish the coaster, flip the loom over and snip the sections of yarn running across the notches. Pair the loose ends and tie them together against the outer rows to create tassels.

Kid-colored Oven Mitts

Making gifts with your kids doesn't get much easier than this. All you need are fabric markers and a child's creativity to turn plain oven mitts and pot holders into handy kitchen art.

MATERIALS

Oven mitt or pot holder
Scrap paper (for practice)
Colored fabric markers (we recommend using Marvy or FabricMate brand pens)

Trace the oven mitt or pot holder onto a sheet of paper so that your child can experiment with different designs — he might try drawing a yellow chick with an orange beak or a spotted dog. Once he has a design, he can resketch it on the oven mitt and carefully color it in with the fabric markers.

Plant Friends

These fuzzy bugs are so cute, they'll be a welcome (and amusing) sight hanging out in anyone's houseplants. Follow the directions below for the ladybug or adjust them slightly to fashion the bumblebee or green fly.

MATERIALS

Black pipe cleaner, cut in half
Small black pom-pom
A large and a mini red pom-pom
Red pipe cleaner, cut in thirds
Multicolored spiraled pipe cleaner
Craft glue
Googly eyes
Thin craft foam (red and black)
Red and white spiraled pipe cleaner
¼-inch wooden dowel, 1 foot long

Create the ladybug's head and body by wrapping one half of the black pipe cleaner around the black and large red pom-poms, securing them together. Twist the ends of the pipe cleaner together under the bug's body (see A).

Slip the three pieces of red pipe cleaner between the black pipe cleaner and pom-poms on the underside of the bug. Bend them to form legs (see B).

For the antennae, slip the multicolored pipe cleaner under the black pipe cleaner on the topside of the bug, just behind the black pom-pom (see C). Twist and shape it, then trim the ends if necessary.

Glue on googly eyes and a red mini pom-pom nose. Then cut a red mouth and black spots out of craft foam and glue them onto the bug.

To attach the bug to the dowel, tightly wrap the red and white pipe cleaner around the top of the dowel and hook the end to the underside of the bug.

Brick Bookends

Painting a brick is the epitome of a simple craft: almost anyone can do it, and no special patterns or materials are required. It also makes an ideal gift for the avid reader in your family.

MATERIALS

Newspaper
Acrylic paints and paintbrushes
Two bricks
Glue and felt

Cover a clean surface with newspaper and set out the acrylic paints and paintbrushes. Stand the bricks vertically, so that your child can paint on her designs. Remember that since the surface of the bricks is porous, it can absorb a good amount of paint. Your child may need to apply several layers to create a solid covering. Or, if she prefers a splotchier effect, as is shown here, stop painting while some of the brick's surface still shows through.

Once the paint dries, trace around the brick bases on felt and cut them out. Glue the felt squares on the bottom of each brick to prevent the brick from scratching your bookshelf or tabletop.

◆ FAMILYFUN READER TRADITION

Holiday Presence

"Instead of buying gifts, each adult in my family picks the name of a child to plan a one-on-one outing for. One brother-in-law took Morgan on a whale watch. Jonathan went to a hockey game with another uncle, and I took my niece to Storyland for the day. What a joy it was to spend less time and money shopping and more time enjoying our families."

— Kelly Vogt, Henniker, New Hampshire

Mosaic Flowerpot

Ronnie Citron-Fink, a *FamilyFun* contributor, has overseen many gift-making sessions, both in her elementary school classroom and with her own two children. This flowerpot project uses broken pottery and old, but treasured, trinkets, creating a useful gift in the process. "At my school, I've made these flowerpots with first graders through sixth graders," says Ronnie, "and even the littlest ones have been able to produce beautifully intricate mosaics."

MATERIALS

Newspaper

Pieces of broken pottery, tiles, beads, marbles, beach glass, shells, or charms

Rubber gloves

Ceramic tile grout (available at hardware stores)

Plastic knife

Terra-cotta flowerpot

Sponge

Cover your work area with newspaper. Before your child starts decorating her pot, sort through the pottery pieces and discard any that have sharp edges (a parent's job). Wearing rubber gloves, spread a heavy layer of tile grout onto the flowerpot with the plastic knife. Press the tile pieces into the wet grout. When you are done making a design, spread a bit more grout between the pieces, so that most of the broken edges are covered. After the pot is dry, wipe off any grout film with a damp sponge.

Tip: If you don't have broken pottery, place chipped, leftover tiles in a clear plastic bag (this way you can see what you're smashing) and break them with a hammer. Another good source for broken tiles is your local tile or hardware store; many will give you broken display tiles for free.

Wishing Stones

For kids who love play clay, making this gift is the perfect project. The stone-colored Sculpey clay is easy to shape into "rock" message signs for gardens and houseplants. Your child can gift-wrap them with a few seed packs or present them in a small potted plant.

MATERIALS

One 1¾-pound box of Sculpey Granitex polymer clay (available at art supply and craft stores)

Toothpicks or a rubber stamp

Aluminum foil

Have your child start with a small piece of the clay, kneading it until it is soft and easy to work with. For a message-bearing rock like our love stone, poke holes with a toothpick to form each letter, then drag the toothpick through the poked holes, or use uninked rubber stamps to print the message. Your child might try printing wishing messages, such as "peace," "smile," or "happiness."

Lay the completed designs on a foil-lined cookie sheet and bake in a preheated 275° oven for 15 minutes per ¼ inch of thickness. Cool on a wire rack. Wrap with a note that says, "Set the wishing stones on the soil in your garden or your houseplants."

✳ **GREETING CARD**

Drying Mittens

What could be homier than a pair of mittens drying on a clothesline? *FamilyFun* reader and kindergarten teacher Maureen Mollette turned this concept into a creative greeting card.

MATERIALS

- 2 sheets of $8^{1}/_{2}$- by 11-inch natural-colored paper, one slightly lighter than the other
- Rubber cement
- Cardboard
- Fabric remnants
- Twine
- Hot glue gun
- Mini clothespins (available at craft supply stores)
- White tissue paper
- White glue

Cut the darker sheet of paper in half to make two cards. Cut to fit the other, lighter-colored sheet, to make the background for the mittens. Glue in place with the rubber cement.

Next, draw a mitten pattern on the cardboard and cut it out to make a template. Trace the template onto the fabric remnants and cut out mittens. Using the hot glue gun (parents only), attach each end of a short length of twine to the card, then clip the mittens to the string with mini clothespins. As a finishing touch, use white glue to attach small squares of white tissue paper "snow" to the bottom of the card.

Gift-wrapped Kids

When *FamilyFun* asked readers for creative holiday card ideas, the Bagnolis of Berea, Kentucky — Lori and Joe and kids Lilianna, Marina, Philip, and Cecelia — sent in this picture featuring the greatest gifts of all.

MATERIALS

Large cardboard boxes
Shiny gift wrap and ribbons
Rubber cement
Paper
Pens, colored pencils, or markers

Start with a cardboard box that is large enough to cover your child's body when seated. Cut out the bottom flaps of the box with a utility knife (parents only). For the head hole, cut out a rectangle on the top of the box that's big enough for your child's head. Cut a box for each of your children.

Enlist your kids to help decorate the boxes with shiny gift wrap. Then have them sit inside the presents and pose for an outdoor photo (with a ribbon on their heads!). Have prints of the photos made, one for each card you plan to send (Lori ordered 100 prints).

Have your children create doodles for the border of the photo on a master card template. Then make copies of the template at a copy shop, and glue the pictures to the cards using rubber

The Season's Greatest Gifts

cement. Lori says that the best part of making this card is that between the doodles and the gift boxes there's plenty of room for kid participation.

Tip: Instead of making prints of each photo, glue one photo to the master template before copying. That way, you won't have to glue copies of the photo to each card.

Punchy Postcards

Send a holiday greeting that showcases your kids' artwork with this fun-to-make postcard craft.

MATERIALS

Paper
Markers, crayons, or colored pencils

Divide a standard sheet of paper into quadrants by folding it in half, then

folding it in half again. Have the kids create festive images in each quadrant using primary colors, which tend to copy better than pastels.

Bring the master to the copy shop and have it color-copied onto card stock. Then, either have the copy shop cut the stack into cards (about $1 per cut) or cut them out yourselves.

Flip the cards over and write your holiday greetings and the recipients' addresses just as you would on regular postcards and stick them in the mail.

THUMBPRINT REINDEER

This whimsical card, sent in by the Persechini family of Overland Park, Kansas, was inspired by the thumbprint art of children's book author and illustrator, Ed Emberley.

MATERIALS

Paper
Ink pads (several colors)
Pens, colored pencils, or markers

Have each family member choose a color and use the ink pads to make several thumbprints on paper. Then draw on antlers, legs, and so forth to make reindeer. The Persechinis scanned their art onto their computer and used Microsoft Greetings to arrange the reindeer and print the cards. You can also hand make each card or have copies made.

Tip: Use your imagination! You can use thumbprints to create Santas, trees, candles, people — you name it.

A Book About Me

Make a kid the hero of his own tale by casting him in a homemade book. This gift is fun for an older child to create for a younger sibling, but would also be nice for you to make for your child. Write a fictionalized story (Julia and the magical pony) or chronicle a milestone (a day in the life of Nicky), then illustrate it with photos and drawings.

MATERIALS

Colored pencils or markers
Scrap and heavy white paper
Photographs
Glue or tape
Hole punch
Ribbon or yarn

Write a simple story line on scrap paper, dividing it into pages. This will help you determine the photographs you need, the length of the book, and the size and shape of the pages. Next, transfer the story with accompanying illustrations and cut-out photos onto the heavy white paper. Leave a ½-inch margin on the side of the paper to be hole-punched. When finished, decorate a cover, stack the pages on top of one another (in order!), and punch two holes along the left margin (three for a standard sheet of paper). Tie yarn or ribbon through the holes for binding.

Tiny Treasure Box

For the collector on your child's gift list, a personalized hobby box is sure to fit the bill. And when your child glues on images of the recipient's favorite things, such as birds for a bird-watcher or movie ticket stubs for a film buff, the real gift becomes the chance to see oneself through the eyes of the giver.

MATERIALS

Small wooden box (available at craft stores)
Acrylic paint (or stain) and paintbrush
Tacky glue
Assorted decorating supplies (items the box will hold, magazine cutouts, photos, wooden or plastic toys)
Nontoxic acrylic sealer and/or Mod Podge

First, apply a light coat of paint or colored stain to the box. While it's drying, your child can pick a theme for the box, such as jungle animals, golf, travel, classical music, cars, or ballet dancing, and choose a bunch of fitting decorations. Our bird theme example, above, would be great for a nature enthusiast. We decorated our box with bird stamps, cutout magazine pictures, and bird stickers.

Have your child glue the decorating supplies he chooses onto the box (and maybe even put a few inside!). We left a lot of the paint showing, but it can be fun to glue images all over the box.

When you're finished, brush on a coat of acrylic sealer or Mod Podge. Lastly, glue a three-dimensional object — say, a golf ball, a plastic toy, or a wooden figurine — to the top of the box.

Sewing Kit

This snazzy felt alligator (aka a sewing kit for pins and needles) is a great gift for the seamstress on your child's list. Does your child have a different animal in mind, like a spotted dog perhaps? She can simply choose other colors and add ears.

MATERIALS

Felt (green, white, and red)
Pinking shears (optional)
Green yarn
Needle
2 green pom-poms
Googly eyes
2 green sequins or beads

Begin by cutting an elongated oval (about 8 by 2 inches) from green felt. From white felt, cut the same shape,

but slightly smaller. Then cut one from red felt that's a bit smaller still. Create jagged teeth around the edge of the white felt by trimming it with pinking shears.

Center the pieces on top of one another (green, white, then red). Fold the stack in half and press it with an iron (a parent's job).

Use the yarn and needle to sew two or three large stitches through the center of the stack of felt to bind the three layers together. Then tie the ends of the yarn into a double knot (on the outside of the alligator) and trim off any excess.

For the alligator's eyes, glue on green pom-poms and googly eyes, and for a snout, glue or sew on the sequins or beads.

Photo Box

This present is just the right size for holding paper clips, tacks, and a million other things. When your child lacquers on a photo of himself and the recipient, the gift becomes not only practical, but also very sentimental.

MATERIALS

Peanut canister (cylindrical cardboard kind with foil lining)
Photographs
Magazine cutouts and stamps
White glue or clear glaze (available at craft stores)

Remove the lid from a clean peanut can. Have your child glue a photo of himself and the recipient onto the plastic lid. Then he can glue magazine pictures, family photos, or even postage stamps onto the sides of the canister. After it dries, paint everything with glaze or white glue that dries clear.

A Pooch's Place Mat

Besides adding a decorative touch to your dog's dinner table (that is, the floor), one of these spongeable potato-print place mats can also make cleaning up spilled kibble a cinch.

MATERIALS

Poster board
Large potato
Bone cookie cutter
Paper towels
Acrylic paints
Paper plates and newspaper
Clear Con-Tact paper

Cut a place mat shape from the poster board. Then, slice the potato in half lengthwise. Press the cookie cutter into the cut surface of the potato half and leave it in place. Pare away a ¼-inch layer of potato from around the cutter (adults only). Remove the cutter and blot the potato with a paper towel.

Pour the paint on a paper plate (use one plate for each color). Now, have your child press the stamp into the paint, dab off any excess color on the newspaper, and press it on the place mat. Rinse and dry the potato before switching to another color. Once his design is dry, laminate the place mat between sheets of clear Con-Tact paper.

✳ QUICK GIFTS

PET PRESENTS

While you're compiling your shopping list this gift-giving season, don't forget Fido! Here are some presents sure to get his tail wagging:

- ✦ A can of tennis balls
- ✦ A nameplate to hang over the door to his house or by his bed
- ✦ His own ornament for the tree
- ✦ A new ID tag
- ✦ A flying disk
- ✦ A wading pool (if it's warm in your area this time of year)
- ✦ A new bowl filled with his favorite treats and toys

And for your favorite feline. . .
- ✦ A homemade catnip sock
- ✦ A scratching post
- ✦ Gourmet cat food
- ✦ A cushy window seat

✻ READY TO WEAR
Fleece Hat

This soft and cozy cap is just the thing to keep your child's best friend or sibling warm in brisk winter weather. In fact, it's so easy to put together (there's just one seam), she could even fashion one for everybody on her list!

MATERIALS
Fleece and cord
Needle and thread
Decorative button or felt cutout

Determine the size of the hat. (To avoid ruining the surprise, measure the head of someone who is similar in size to the recipient.) Cut a piece of fleece that's 16 inches wide and as long as the measurement you took plus 2 inches.

Fold the fleece in half right side in so the 16-inch edges match up. Sew a ½-inch-wide seam along this edge, stopping 5 inches from the bottom (see A). Just below the last stitch, make a ½-inch cut in from the side. Turn the material right side out. Now, sew a seam along the last 5 inches of unsewn fleece (see B).

Roll the bottom of the hat up two turns, so the cuff conceals the bottom part of the seam. To keep the cuff from unrolling, sew on a decorative button or a felt cutout.

Finally, gather the top 3 inches of the hat and tie a colorful cord around it.

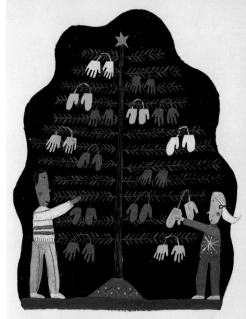

✻ THE GIVING SPIRIT
TRIM A MITTEN TREE

Winter can be one of the hardest times for disadvantaged families, and a clothing drive can help relieve some of that burden. Talk to someone from your town's community center, a church, or even a local business about setting up a holiday tree for the public to trim with mittens, scarves, and hats. Then, donate the offerings to a local shelter or another charitable organization that can distribute them.

✻ READY TO WEAR
Sweater Mittens

Made from old sweaters that have been "felted" (shrunken into a dense, nonraveling material), these mittens are soft, toasty, and very colorful. They cost almost nothing to make and are a nice way to recycle your stretched-out, old sweaters into lovely and useful gifts.

MATERIALS
Old wool sweater (you must use 100 percent wool; tight weaves work especially well)
Pins
Yarn
Tapestry or yarn needle

Wash the sweater in the hot cycle of your washer three or four times with your regular detergent. Then pop the sweater into the dryer for about 45 minutes, or until it shrinks and becomes feltlike in texture. Certain sweaters, you'll find, shrink better than others, and the drying time will vary, depending on the sweater's thickness.

To make a mitten template, trace around one of your (or your child's) mittens, leaving an extra inch or so around the edge for sewing. Pin the template onto the felted fabric, then cut out four matching mitten shapes.

Pin two of the mitten sides together. Using a contrasting color of yarn, stitch around the edges (a blanket stitch, as we've used here, looks especially attractive). Leftover felt can be used to make purses, eyeglass cases, doll clothes, or even a dog collar.

Tip: If you don't have any old wool sweaters, check at a local thrift shop (they rarely charge more than two or three dollars per sweater). Keep an eye out for old Fair Isles; the intricate patterns shrink into pretty designs.

✳ HANDMADE FOR THE HOME
Foamy Frame

This funky foam frame is simple enough for little fingers yet offers limitless personalizing possibilities for older kids. In addition to making the basic square, kids can cut the foam into a Christmas tree or a wreath.

MATERIALS

One 9- by 12-inch sheet of craft foam
Flexible pocket magnet frame (we used Original Soft Pocket Magnetic Photo Frames by Lytle, available in 3½ by 5, 4 by 6, and 5 by 7 inches)
Hot glue gun
Assorted accessories such as beads, buttons, fake jewels, glitter, googly eyes, or prepackaged foam cutouts
Photo

Cut a shape slightly smaller than the magnetic photo frame from the center of the foam sheet. Be sure the inside edge of the foam frame overlaps the magnetic frame by at least ¼ inch. Next, apply a thin line of hot glue to one edge of the magnetic frame's clear front and firmly press the foam frame in place. Repeat with the remaining edges, one at a time, being careful not to glue over the pocket's opening. Trim the frame, leaving a margin of foam for covering the outer edge of the magnetic frame. Glue on decorative accessories and slip a favorite photo into the pocket.

✳ PERSONALIZED PRESENT
Picture Brooches

Who needs to show off diamonds when you've got heirloom jewels like these? Grandparents will be especially thrilled and proud to wear these beautiful brooches on their lapels. The craft also presents them with the opportunity to talk about the creative lads and lassies who made them: their grandchildren.

MATERIALS

Needle-nose pliers
Bottle cap
Pin backing (available at craft stores)
White glue or clear glaze (available at craft stores)
Nail polish and glitter
Photo

To make your pin, use needle-nose pliers to bend out and flatten the rim of a bottle cap (parents only). Then glue a pin backing to the cap. Let your child decorate the inside edge of the cap with nail polish and glued-on glitter. Next, have her trace a quarter around a photo of her choice and cut it out. Finally, glue the picture in the center of the bottle cap and coat it with clear glaze or white glue that dries clear.

Photo Books

Filled with your favorite photos, this is just the present for a relative or special friend. At first glance, it looks like an album, but open it into a full circle, tie the ribbon binding it into a bow, and it's ready to display on an end table.

MATERIALS

- 7 family photos
- Craft knife
- 4-ply and 2-ply rag board (used for matting artwork and sold at most art supply stores)
- 26-inch-long piece of ribbon
- Colored paper
- Glue stick

Use a craft knife to cut two 5- by 6½-inch rectangles from the 4-ply rag board for the book covers. For the inner pages, cut one 5- by 39-inch rectangle from the 2-ply rag board. With your child, lightly mark 6½-inch increments along the long edges of the 2-ply rag board and accordion-fold the sheet at those marks (see A). Use a ruler edge to press the folds into sharp creases.

Lay the ribbon on a tabletop and center the folded rag board on top so that the side with three creases is on the left and lines up with the midpoint of the ribbon (see B). Apply glue to the top of the folded rag board. Then lay the left side of the ribbon over the glued page (see C) and top with one of the book covers, pressing firmly until well stuck. Flip over the book and use the same method to attach the right side of the ribbon and the back cover.

Now cut the colored paper into seven 4- by 5½-inch rectangles. Glue one onto the center of each page and the front cover; then glue the photos onto the colored paper.

On the Ball

True, *FamilyFun* **reader** Ric Brown is a professional photographer. But, says his wife, Kim, "This card is something anybody can do at home." Here's how.

MATERIALS

- Tripod and camera
- Christmas ball
- Glue stick
- Construction paper

To create the fun-house effect of their Christmas card, the Browns — including daughter Tessa, age seven — set up a regular, everyday camera on a tripod and photographed their reflection in a silver Christmas ball. No special lighting. No special equipment.

After the photos came back, they used a glue stick to cover the back of each photo with construction paper, cut out the balls, then wrote their greeting on the flip sides. Recipients gave the card rave reviews. "We'd go over to visit people, and it would be hanging on their tree," says Kim. "It's on a few refrigerators still. Everyone got a laugh, and that's really the point, to me — to say, 'we're here,' and keep it nice and light."

Votive Candleholders

Decorating votive candleholders offers an hour's worth of activity for your child and a winter's worth of light and warmth for the recipient.

MATERIALS
Assorted colors of tissue paper
White glue
Paintbrush
Small glass jar or votive candleholder
Votive candle

To make a candleholder, your child should first cut or tear pieces of colored tissue paper into stripes, spots, flowers, and other festive shapes or designs.

Then help her glue the tissue paper onto the glass jar or candleholder in a design she likes (a brush makes applying the white glue easier). Keep in mind that overlapping the different colors creates a stained-glass effect that's especially pretty. After the design dries, put a votive candle in each holder.

✳ HANDMADE FOR THE HOME

Beauty Bar

Even the most exotic of bath accessories will take a backseat to this one-of-a-kind soap created by a young artist. Be forewarned, though — your children will find this craft addictive. Buy many bars of soap and expect your relatives to be exceptionally clean in the coming year.

MATERIALS
Bar of soap
Acrylic paints and paintbrushes
Aluminum coffee can
Large pot
Canning wax or a white candle

Have your children paint designs on the soap with the acrylic paint. Meanwhile, you should create a double boiler by putting the coffee can in a pot half-filled with water. Drop in wax and melt it over low heat. Then use a disposable paintbrush to cover the design on top of the soap. Let the wax dry. The protective coating will allow the soap to be used without washing away the picture.

Handprint Apron

When her daughter, Heather, was in preschool, Nancy Ojeda of Houston helped the class make a handprint apron for their teacher. On their way to the bus, the four-year-olds lined up in the parking lot, dipped their hands in saucers of paint, and pressed them on the apron. "It went like clockwork," she says. When they were done, the apron was covered with 16 little handprints. Nancy appreciated how easy it was to make the gift. What did the kids like? "Oh, the mess!"

MATERIALS
- Newspaper
- Solid-colored apron
- Fabric paints
- Paper plates
- Fabric pen

Cover a work area with newspaper and lay the apron right side up. Pour paint into a paper plate. Your kids can press their hands in the paint, move them around until the palm sides are covered, then place their handprints on the apron. Continue until the apron is covered with prints. Write each child's name with a fabric pen under his handprint. Let dry at least one day before wearing.

★ HANDMADE FOR THE HOME

House Keys

Getting out of the house is hard enough on most days, but it becomes decidedly more challenging when keys are misplaced. This handy housekey holder makes a decorative (and practical!) gift for a busy relative or friend.

MATERIALS
- Wooden blocks (available at craft stores)
- Carpenter's wood glue
- Acrylic paints and paintbrushes
- Cup hooks
- Picture frame hanger

Together with your child, use blocks and wood glue to create a small-scale replica of the recipient's house (or neighborhood). Your child can then paint it with acrylics, again using the actual one (Grammy's cottage or Uncle Dave's apartment) as a model.

Along the bottom of the house (or houses), screw in cup hooks. Finally, affix a picture frame hanger on the back so the key holder can hang on a nail.

✴ GREETING CARD
A Pine Pin

These holiday cards offer two gifts in one: a greeting and a Christmas tree pin for the recipient to wear.

MATERIALS

    4- by 8-inch piece of green card stock
    Glitter glue and puffy paint
    Glue
    Pin backing
    White card stock
    Red tissue paper
    Sticker star

Begin by having your child decorate the green card stock with glitter glue and puffy paint. When the card is dry, sketch a row of simple tree shapes on the back. Cut out the trees and glue a pin backing to each one.

Next, fold sheets of white card stock in half horizontally and glue a piece of red tissue paper to the front of each, as shown. Cut a slit (long enough to accommodate the pin backing) in the center of the card front and slip the pin in place as pictured. Add a sticker star above the tree, write your message inside, and your card is ready to be hand-delivered.

✴ READY TO WEAR
Snowman T-shirts

This holiday season, let it snow on these whimsical winter shirts. Because the snow is made with bleach, be sure to supervise the craft closely, work in a ventilated room, wear rubber gloves, and remind your kids to use caution.

MATERIALS

    Brightly colored cotton T-shirt, prewashed
    Plastic trash bag or old plastic tablecloth
    Plastic grocery bags
    3 kitchen sponges
    Rubber gloves
    Bleach and spray bottle
    Empty margarine tub or other container
    Fabric markers

Lay the shirt flat on the trash bag and slip one or two grocery bags flat inside it. Cut the sponges into a star and two circles, one slightly larger than the other. Rinse them with water and wring them out thoroughly.

With a window open for ventilation, and wearing the rubber gloves, pour a shallow layer of bleach into the margarine tub and about 2 inches into the spray bottle. Spritz bleach across the bottom of the shirt to saturate it. Gradually apply less bleach as you move up the shirt, ending with a thin mist across the middle. Allow the bleach to soak in for a moment to see how it's working.

Tip: If the bleached areas are not easily seen, you can mark the bleached (snow) and unbleached (sky) portions of the shirt with masking tape to avoid losing your snowman in a blizzard!

For the snowman, dip the larger round sponge into the bleach, squeezing out excess liquid, then press it onto the shirt. Check the boldness of the imprint and repeat this step if necessary, but avoid using too much bleach. Repeat with the smaller round sponge for the snowman's head, then finish off with a bleached star. Allow the shirt to dry overnight, then soak it briefly in hot, soapy water, and rinse. Once dried, use the fabric markers to add the snowman's buttons and facial features.

Holiday Surprise Box

When the Hampson family moved to Round Rock, Texas, several years ago, they suddenly faced a 2,000-mile gap between themselves and their cousins. Their Christmas box — the Hampsons' clever way of bridging the distance during the holidays — became a heartfelt gift, one that just might bring comfort and joy to your family as well.

MATERIALS

- Cylindrical cardboard box (available at craft supply stores)
- Local treasures, such as postcards and nature finds
- Kids' artwork and photos
- Raffia ribbon

Have your kids collect items that tell a story about where you live and the lives you lead there: seashells, pressed flowers, pinecones, postcards with a local theme, edible items, trading cards, ticket stubs — anything that says "me" and "mine." (Don't forget drawings and photos.) Have your kids carefully package these items into the cardboard box and tie with a ribbon.

Tip: Suggest to your relatives that you would like to make the box a reciprocal affair: while your kids are assembling one for their cousins upstate, their cousins will be putting together a similar box for them.

Kid's Art Notepad

Take a favorite drawing, add the services of a copy shop, and you'll be amazed at the results. Your child's art can be copied, cut, and bound into a useful notepad, allowing even the youngest gifter to create a treasured present for a teacher or grandparent.

MATERIALS

- Kid's artwork (made with a black marker)
- White-out tape (available at copy shops)
- Magnetic tape (optional)

Help your child make a line drawing with a black marker. She might try a stick-figure family portrait, a snowman, or a tree (she can also include her name or the name of the recipient). Bring her artwork to a copy shop and reduce the image to a 1½-inch square. Make four copies and cut out the images. Fold a piece of paper into quarters, unfold, then tape an image onto the top of each quarter (use white-out tape to hide the edges). Using this as a master, have the copy shop make four 100-sheet notepads with cardboard backing (approximately $12 to $18). If you wish, add a strip of magnetic tape to the backing to create a refrigerator pad.

Toy Workshop

Put your little elves to work and, in the process, redirect their preholiday energy toward giving as well as getting. Set aside a day during the holidays to transform your playroom into Santa's workshop. Unlike the original at the North Pole, yours won't be turning out new toys but recycling old ones — all those outgrown, no-longer-beloved playthings.

MATERIALS

> Your kids' outgrown toys, dolls, and
> other playthings
> Damp dust rag
> White glue
> Hairbrush and ribbons
> Ziplock bags

Have each of your kids select a few old toys to rejuvenate and give to a needy child. They won't be doing any major surgery; truly broken toys should be given a solemn farewell and tossed in the trash. But for the rest, have on hand a damp dust rag (for spiffing up grimy plastic), a bottle of white glue (for attaching googly eyes to a puppet), and a hairbrush and ribbons (for dressing up old dolls). Using ziplock bags, your kids can collect small items like doll clothes and action figures and even assemble special themed packages, such as an outer space set made up of miniature aliens, toy rocket ships, and glow-in-the-dark stars or a rain forest pack of plastic jungle animals.

When all the toys are groomed and ready to go, arrange to donate them to kids in need: contact local shelters, church groups, and civic organizations to find out how. Your elves will take pride in a good deed well done.

Emoticon Magnets

Here's a fun gift idea for the computer buff on your child's list: turn those quirky keyboard symbols that express feeling in cyberspace into funny-faced refrigerator magnets. The ones shown here were made with some of the more familiar "emoticons," or "smileys." Check the sheet above for possibilities or encourage your child to see what other expressions she can create.

MATERIALS

> Computer and printer
> Colored markers
> Clear, flat decorative gems
> Glue
> Small, round self-adhesive magnets

Use your computer to create a variety of emoticon faces slightly smaller than the gems. Leave plenty of space between them. When you have enough, print them out.

Use the markers to decorate and color in the faces. Then cut out the faces, trimming them into ovals or circles slightly smaller than the gems.

Glue each cutout (facedown) to the back of a glass pebble and then affix a magnet. Make sure the glue dries completely before you wrap the magnets as a gift.

Put-On-a-Show Kit

Sure, lots of stores sell kits, but none of those are custom-assembled with the insider knowledge and special touches that only a close friend or sibling would know to add. This dramatic play kit — a hatbox loaded with everything the recipient needs to stage a play fit for Broadway, or at least Grandfather's house — was assembled for six-year-old Koko, the daughter of *FamilyFun* contributor Shoshana Marchand.

MATERIALS

Vintage clothes, boas, belts, and hats
Costume jewelry
Face paint or masks
Tickets
Popcorn

Check out vintage clothing stores for boas, belts, and costume jewelry. Then hit the party store and load up on drama staples such as a sheriff's badge and face paints. You can also scour around the attic for some scarves and accessories from your younger years.

Give the kit a finishing touch by adding tickets for the kids to "sell" and popcorn to serve. This kit is also an excellent group gift.

More Custom Kit Ideas

Chocolate Chip Cookie Kit: Fill a large, clear mixing bowl with all kinds of goodies for learning to bake — including a homemade certificate from Mom or Dad, promising chocolate chip cookie baking lessons.

First Tool Kit: Raid the hardware store for a beginner's collection of tools (hammer, nails, safety goggles, and so on), then pack them into a small toolbox or tool belt. Add some hunks of wood and a card that lists safety rules.

Junior Executive Kit: Use an old briefcase to hold a calculator, Post-its, a notebook, pens, paper clips, and other supplies for a booming business.

Print with Pears

Even though practicality sometimes calls for us parents to choose and pay for holiday gifts, *FamilyFun* editor Cindy Littlefield says there's still plenty of room for our kids to get in on the act. With a little paint and a pear, for instance, kids can stamp an unwrapped box into a stunning package that equals two presents in one.

MATERIALS
Acrylic paint
Paper plate
Pear (that's not too ripe)
Paper towel
Unwrapped white box or white paper

Spread some paint on the paper plate. (The shade shown here was created by mixing green, white, and yellow paints.) Use a paring knife to slice the pear vertically into halves (a parent's job) so that the stem remains attached to one half. Blot dry the cut surfaces with a paper towel.

Press a pear half, cut side down, into the paint and then onto the box or paper (you may want to practice on scrap paper first). Repeat to create a pattern or a random design. Or try experimenting with different colors. Let the paint dry completely before attaching a ribbon or a gift tag.

Gift Wrap on the Road

"Facing a 16-hour road trip at Christmastime, we wanted to ensure our young daughter was entertained. However, we knew that our fully packed car would not allow room for many playthings. Since much of our cargo was gifts, I wrapped them in plain white paper and let Hope decorate them with crayons and markers as we traveled. She stayed busy and had fun, and the recipients loved the special wrapping."

— Carol Marion
Nashville, Tennessee

Frosty the Envelope

With this simple painting technique, your child can take a large envelope, give it character, and call it a wrap for a gift book, puzzle, or video.

MATERIALS
Mailing envelope (11 by 17 inches)
Construction paper and masking tape
Soft sponge
Blue tempera paint
Markers, felt, and white glue

Cut a snowman shape from construction paper and use a few pieces of rolled masking tape to stick it temporarily to the face of the envelope.

Dip the sponge into the blue paint and then dab color onto the envelope all around the snowman. Let dry.

Carefully remove the paper cutout and then use colored markers to draw a face, arms, a hat, and buttons. Finally, glue on a miniature felt scarf.

✳ GREETING CARD

Hanukkah Hands

This "handmade" Hanukkah card was inspired by the tiny fingers of *FamilyFun* reader Lauri Levenberg's two-year-old daughter Brielle. "I realized that they would be perfect for the shape of a menorah," says Lauri.

MATERIALS

 Blue construction paper
 Glue
 Sheet of heavy paper
 Gold glitter crayon

 Trace your child's hands onto the blue construction paper, overlapping the thumbs to make the shammes candle in the middle. Then fold the heavy paper in half and glue the paper cutout onto one side. Finally, "light" the flames with a gold glitter crayon.

✳ GREETING CARD

Photo Booth Card

This card was more "desperation than inspiration," admits *FamilyFun* reader Jami Champagne. She and her husband, Brian, had always sent out cards with a family photo. But there was no time for a formal portrait when Brian was in grad school and working full-time. So, she gathered her brood and opted for this fun photo booth card.

MATERIALS

 Assorted photos from a photo booth
 White paper
 Glue
 Star stamp and gold ink pad

 At the photo booth, take as many strips as needed to get a half dozen good and varied photos. Bring the photos home and create a master sheet for photocopying. You might divide the sheet in half and cut and arrange the photos to create two folded cards (as shown). Or, divide a standard sheet of paper into thirds, glue a photo strip to each column, and create three skinny postcards per sheet that fit nicely into business size envelopes. Color-copy the final design and stamp it with gold stars.

✳ FAMILYFUN READER IDEA

FULL HOUSE

Last year Mindy d'Arbeloff decided it was time to pass the card-making torch to her four-year-old daughter, Chardy. So, she asked her to paint a picture of their home. When it was done, they picked out their favorite photos of each other — and dad Jim Peyser, baby Rubye, and pet cat Gracie — trimmed them down to silhouettes, and glued them into the windows. With a mailing list approaching 200, the family found color-copying was the costliest part of this project (about $1 per card). Still, Mindy wouldn't have it any other way. "People still tell me they couldn't bring themselves to throw it out," she says.

✳ GREETING CARD
Family Tree

The Christmas *FamilyFun* reader Connie Singer had three kids under five, she said she figured it was "a hand-print kind of year" — a trend she put to use in the making of this card.

THE SINGER FAMILY TREE

MATERIALS
- Paper plate
- Green tempera paint
- Sheets of white paper
- Double-sided tape
- Markers

Pour the paint onto the paper plate. Have each child stamp his hands into the paint and then onto the paper. Don't try to make a design, just try to get a print that is clear and not smeared. Once you have some usable prints, let them dry and have them reduced at a copy shop. Then, cut them out and arrange them on a separate sheet of paper to make a tree (use double-sided tape to ensure that the artwork stays smooth and flat, thus avoiding shadows). Draw on a square trunk filling in the year. You can spare the family pets the inking, but do draw in their prints so they won't be left out. Finally, color-copy the final design.

✳ GREETING CARD
Christmas Stamp Cards

Jack, the six-year-old son of *FamilyFun*'s editorial director Alix Kennedy, wanted to draw the family holiday cards last year. Because they planned to send out more than 100 cards, Alix knew it would be impossible for him to draw each one. Instead, she converted one of Jack's drawings, his holiday greeting, and his signature into rubber stamps at an office supply store. In one short evening, they stamped each card. Jack got many wonderful messages of appreciation back from family friends, but what Alix loved most is that now she has three rubber stamps that so beautifully capture her kindergartner's drawings and handwriting.

MATERIALS
- Scrap paper and markers
- Blank cards and envelopes
- Ink pad

Have your child draw a holiday picture, such as a snowman or reindeer, on scrap paper. Keep in mind that line drawings produce the best results. Then, have him handwrite a holiday greeting and sign his name. Next, photocopy all three, reducing them each to a size that fits the cards nicely.

Drop the copies off at a local office supply, copy, or printing shop and have them converted into three rubber stamps. (It was a five-day wait for Alix and Jack, and the stamps cost about $40 for all three.)

When you get the stamps back, have your child stamp each of the blank cards with all three stamps.

Tip: For her cards and envelopes, Alix purchased soft, thick ivory stationery from an art supply store.

Handy Tags

Add a personalized touch to the gifts your family offers this season with handmade mitten tags.

MATERIALS

- Child-size mittens
- Poster board
- Colored or decorative paper
- Hole punch and ribbon

To make a tag, have your kids trace around child-size mittens onto poster board. Or they can hold their hands down on the paper, fingers together, while you trace around them. Now cut out the shapes and use them as templates to trace onto colored or decorative paper. Cut out each paper mitten and punch a hole through the cuff. Then thread a ribbon through the hole for attaching the inscribed tag to a present.

Gift Wrap Station

This clever ribbon dispenser makes it a cinch for kids to lend a hand decorating your gift boxes. Plus, it doubles as a convenient storage place for wrapping paper scraps, gift tags, and tape.

MATERIALS

- Cardboard box with a cover (the kind shoes or work boots come in)
- Gift wrap scraps and glue or tape
- Craft knife
- $3/8$ inch wooden dowel (cut 2 inches longer than the width of the box)

Have your child decorate the outside of the box by gluing or taping on pieces of festive gift wrap. Next, make matching holes in opposite sides of the box to fit the dowel (a parent's job). Insert the dowel through one hole partway into the box, then slide on reels of decorating ribbon and push the dowel end out the opposite hole. (Wrap a rubber band around each end of the dowel to keep it from sliding back through, if needed.) Now make holes in the box front and thread the ribbon ends through them.

♦ **FAMILYFUN READER TRADITION**

Ribbon-cutting Ceremony

"On the night before Christmas, I hang a big red bow across the door to our family room with long streamers that reach from one side of the door frame to the other. On

Christmas morning, each family member gets a pair of scissors (which I have placed on the floor in front of the ribbon the previous night), and we all cut the ribbon at the same time. No one is allowed in the family room until the ribbon is cut. Only then do we all go in and open presents.

This has been our tradition for 13 years. One year, we even found our two youngest children asleep beneath the ribbon waiting for us to cut it."

— Connie Stewart
Tulsa, Oklahoma

Present Scents

Looking for a fun way to spice up your holiday gift packages? With the following easy craft project, you and your kids can adorn them with seasonal cutouts that double as fragrant (but nonedible!) tree ornaments.

MATERIALS

1 cup applesauce (not the chunky variety)
1 1/2 cups ground cinnamon
1/3 cup white glue
Plastic drinking straw
Cookie cutters
Ribbon

In a mixing bowl, stir together the applesauce, cinnamon, and white glue. Form the mixture into a ball, wrap it in plastic, and chill for at least 30 minutes until the "dough" stiffens.

Sprinkle more cinnamon on a cutting board or a waxed-paper-lined surface and turn the chilled dough onto it. Dust a rolling pin with cinnamon and use it to roll out the dough to a 1/4-inch thickness (if it's thinner than that, the ornaments will be too fragile). Cut out decorative shapes with assorted cookie cutters or a butter knife, then use a plastic drinking straw to make a hole through the top center of each cutout.

Place the shapes on a cooling rack and allow them to dry for about two days. The color, which is a deep brown when the dough is wet, will lighten significantly. Finally, fashion a hanger for each ornament by looping a piece of colored ribbon through the hole.

Sponge Print Paper

With paint and sponges, it's easy to mass-produce stacks of bright and striking wrapping papers and gift tags. Simple for kids to cut into shapes, the sponges are safe alternatives to cutting potatoes for prints — and they can be rinsed out and used again.

MATERIALS

Tempera or acrylic paints
Paper plates
Kitchen sponges
Shelf, butcher, or tissue paper
Hole punch
Ribbon

Pour each paint color into a separate paper plate. Use scissors to cut holiday shapes, such as trees, stars, or hearts, out of the slightly dampened sponges. Now your children can dip the sponges into the paint and press them as evenly as possible onto the plain paper, then repeat to create different patterns. Before pressing the sponge into a new paint color, rinse it out in the sink (so the colors won't mix). Let the paper dry before using it to wrap your gifts.

To make gift tags, cut the paper into a square a little larger than your design. Stamp the sponge onto the paper card. Once dry, punch a hole in the top corner of the tag, thread with a ribbon, and attach it to the gift.

Index

Pinecone Trees, page 9

Popsicle-stick Snowflake, page 15

PHOTOGRAPHERS

Robert Benson: 26

Paul Berg: 61

Peter Fox: 22 (top), 72 (bottom)

Jim Gipe: 81 (bottom), 90, 91 (left)

Andrew Greto: 43 (bottom), 46 (bottom), 48 (right), 50 (top right)

Jacqueline Hopkins: 32, 35 (bottom), 37 (top), 40 (left), 42 (top, bottom left), 44, 46 (top), 47 (bottom), 49, 50 (top left and bottom), 52 (middle, bottom left)

Tom Hopkins: 6, 8, 15 (top), 18 (bottom), 56 (top), 59 (middle left)

Ed Judice: Front cover (cover image, top right, top left), 3 (top and bottom right), 5, 7, 9 (top middle, bottom right), 10 (bottom), 11, 12, 13, 14, 17 (left), 19, 21, 22 (bottom), 23 (top), 24 (right), 25 (bottom right), 27, 28, 30, 31, 33, 39 (top and middle), 42 (bottom right), 43 (top, middle), 45 (top left, bottom), 52 (bottom right), 54, 55, 57 (top), 58 (top), 60, 63 (top), 64 (top), 66 (top left), 68, 69, 70, 71, 72 (top), 73, 74, 75, 76, 77, 78 (left), 79 (top left, bottom), 80, 81 (top), 82, 83, 84, 85, 86, 87, 88, 89, 92, 93 (left), 94 (bottom), 96 (top), Back cover (top left, bottom right, bottom)

Kelly-Mooney Photography/CORBIS: 63 (bottom)

Lightworks Photographic: Front cover (bottom left), 18 (top), 20, 24 (left)

Marcy Maloy: 23 (bottom), 29

Mark Mantegna: 56 (middle, bottom), 67 (bottom)

Joanne Schmaltz: Front cover (bottom right), 9 (bottom right), 10 (top, middle), 15 (bottom), 16, 25 (top right), 35 (top), 38, 39 (bottom), 40 (right), 41 (middle and bottom), 45 (top right), 91 (right), 94 (top), 95

Shaffer/Smith Photography: 3 (bottom left), 17 (right), 34, 36, 37 (bottom), 41 (top), 45 (middle right), 47 (top), 48 (left), 51, 52 (top), 53, 57 (bottom left), 59 (top, middle right), 62 (bottom), 65, 66 (top right, bottom), Back cover (top and middle right)

Silver Photography: 93 (top)

Edwina Stevenson: 4, 67 (top)

Team Russell: 78 (right)

Caroline W. Woodham: 58 (bottom)

Jake Wyman: 62 (top)

ILLUSTRATORS

Douglas Bantz: 10, 25, 26, 79 (middle), 81

David Frampton: 63

Linda Helton: 79 (right)

Bruce Macpherson: 64

Holly, Jolly Apron,
page 70

Also from FamilyFun

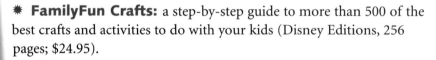

* **FamilyFun magazine:** a creative guide to all the great things families can do together. Call 800-289-4849 for a subscription.

* **FamilyFun Cookbook:** a collection of more than 250 irresistible recipes for you and your kids, from healthy snacks to birthday cakes to dinners everyone in the family can enjoy (Disney Editions, 256 pages; $24.95).

* **FamilyFun Crafts:** a step-by-step guide to more than 500 of the best crafts and activities to do with your kids (Disney Editions, 256 pages; $24.95).

* **FamilyFun Parties:** a complete party planner featuring 100 celebrations for birthdays, holidays, and every day (Disney Editions, 224 pages; $24.95).

* **FamilyFun Cookies for Christmas:** a batch of 50 recipes for creative holiday treats (Disney Editions; 64 pages; $9.95).

* **FamilyFun Tricks and Treats:** a collection of wickedly easy crafts, costumes, party plans, and recipes for Halloween (Disney Editions, 98 pages; $14.95).

* **FamilyFun Boredom Busters:** a collection of 365 activities, from instant fun and after school crafts to kitchen projects and learning games (Disney Editions, 224 pages; $24.95).

* **FamilyFun.com:** visit us at www.familyfun.com and search our extensive archives for games, crafts, recipes, and holiday projects.